Advance Praise

"What makes for a competent board and competent board members in a world in which the old mantra of shareholder value maximization is no longer viable? Helle Bank Jorgensen has thought long and fruitfully on this question. Her book gives invaluable guidance on what boards must do if the businesses they guide are to respond successfully to today's enormous economic, environmental, and social challenges."

MARTIN WOLF,
CHIEF ECONOMICS COMMENTATOR, FINANCIAL TIMES

"I wish I had read this book many years ago ... Not many have the insight and foresight of Helle Bank Jorgensen to see the risks and opportunities of the future that will help you ask the right questions."

CHAD HOLLIDAY,
CHAIR OF THE MISSION POSSIBLE PARTNERSHIP;
FORMER CHAIR, ROYAL DUTCH SHELL AND
BANK OF AMERICA

"*Stewards of the Future* brings a fresh approach on the new set of responsibilities that board members face in this fast-paced, ever-evolving environment, where the planet and segments of the society that were overlooked before occupy a much more relevant role. Through practical examples, guides, and real-life experiences, this book will help any leader who wants to keep up with new environmental, ethical, financial, and societal demands."

CLAUDIA SENDER,
NON-EXECUTIVE DIRECTOR OF SEVERAL PROMINENT
EUROPEAN AND BRAZILIAN COMPANIES

"In this book, Helle Bank Jorgensen has succeeded in bringing an extra dimension to the ESG and sustainability discussions in the boardroom. Helle has achieved this through her 30-year personal passion and vast network, bringing the topic closer to corporate DNA. This is a book not just for board directors but for anyone who is interested in creating a better future for all."

MAY TAN,
INED CLP HOLDINGS AND LINK REIT;
FORMER CEO -STANDARD CHARTERED BANK (HK)

"In this book, Helle Bank Jorgensen provides boards with insights on how to deal with several of the most challenging issues of our time and how to anchor long-termism, addressing SDGs and balancing ESG in the board."

FEIKE SIJBESMA,
FORMER CEO ROYAL DSM; BOARD DIRECTOR,
UNILEVER AND PHILIPS

"Governance is one of the most important drivers of long-term value creation. *Stewards of the Future* highlights this critical issue and helps boards focus on what matters."

SARAH KEOHANE WILLIAMSON,
CHIEF EXECUTIVE OFFICER,
FCLTGLOBAL

"*Stewards of the Future* makes a compelling case to ensure that Stakeholder Capitalism and ESG are integrated into every modern boardroom and corporation in order to better serve all stakeholders."

MARK HAWKINS,
PRESIDENT AND CFO EMERITUS,
SALESFORCE

"This book is a culmination of the most important duty of today's boards as told through the voices of thousands of business leaders the author has encountered while raising awareness on this important subject."

EMILY WAITA MACHARIA,
AFRICA PUBLIC AFFAIRS DIRECTOR,
COCA-COLA AFRICA

"If businesses are willing to look to the horizon, they will see a wave forming. It is made up of multiple sharpening challenges, from cries for social justice to global pandemics to the climate crisis. When that wave crests in a matter of years, not decades, it will drown many businesses who are treading water in the status quo. Some, however, might just learn how to catch the wave and help solve these challenges. For corporate directors, this book is your surfboard. Read it, and then start paddling."

JOHN A. LANIER,
EXECUTIVE DIRECTOR,
RAY C. ANDERSON FOUNDATION

"*Stewards of the Future* is a must-read for everyone in business. An engaging and comprehensive guidebook packed with practical advice and enlightening stories from some of the world's best-known business leaders, *Stewards of the Future* couldn't be more timely. ESG pioneer Helle Bank Jorgensen does a terrific job of sharing the courageous, innovative, empathetic, and ultimately rewarding journeys every business leader must take to create real long-term value for people and planet."

AMANDA ELLIS,
EXECUTIVE DIRECTOR, ASIA-PACIFIC, ASU GLOBAL
INSTITUTE OF SUSTAINABILITY AND INNOVATION

"Helle Bank Jorgensen brilliantly describes the evolution of ESG to its current place of prominence in boardrooms and makes a powerful case for how it will drive value creation. A must-read for all directors and executives seeking to navigate these turbulent times."

MICHAEL KOBORI,
CHIEF SUSTAINABILITY OFFICER, STARBUCKS

"When we leave this earth, as we all inevitably must, what matters will be what we leave behind and for whose benefit. Ten conscience questions per chapter and eleven chapters later, you will know what your company should leave behind and for whom."

R. GOPALAKRISHNAN,
AUTHOR AND CORPORATE ADVISOR;
FORMER DIRECTOR AT TATA GROUP

"An exceptional book for all Board members who serve as custodians of the corporate culture and as leaders who need to build immediate and future trust and confidence in their company and loyalty from their staff. It should be standard reading for all Board members, 'experienced' or not."

HUGUETTE LABELLE,
CHAIR, INTERNATIONAL ANTI-CORRUPTION
CONFERENCE

"If I had just one person to guide me in being a better director, it would be Helle. Her breadth and depth of experience and her leadership in meeting head-on the complex challenges of the day is unmatched. *Stewards of the Future* should be required board reading."

ERIC WETLAUFER,
DIRECTOR, TMX GROUP AND INVESTMENT MANAGEMENT
CORPORATION OF ONTARIO (IMCO)

"*Stewards of the Future* is a tool and guide for board members to be excellent leaders who guide and develop companies that create legacies beyond financial results. Who wouldn't want to be part of something that impactful?"

MAIREAD LAVERY,
PRESIDENT & CEO,
EXPORT DEVELOPMENT CANADA

"This book provides all you need to know to be inspired as a Board member, current, past, and future. Business must step up as climate change has no vaccine and we cannot socially distance ourselves from inequality. Helle's book shows how business leaders can contribute to saving the world."

PAUL DRUCKMAN,
CHAIR, WORLD BENCHMARKING ALLIANCE;
FOUNDING CEO, INTERNATIONAL INTEGRATED
REPORTING COUNCIL

"As a senior fund manager, I would suggest this book as a must-read for all potential and existing public listed board members."

SHIREEN MUHIUDEEN,
FOUNDER, CORSTON-SMITH
ASSET MANAGEMENT

"Climate, diversity, and other ESG issues have moved into the core of the boardroom. Learn and get inspired by Helle Bank Jorgensen's great book."

TORBEN MÖGER PEDERSEN,
CEO, PENSIONDANMARK

"A book about the future role and responsibilities of the board of directors could not be more timely. If that book is written by Helle Bank Jorgensen, based on her thirty years of experience advising companies and investors on ESG, climate, and sustainability, that book will be a bestseller."

ANNETTE VERSCHUREN, O.C.,
CHAIR AND CEO, NRSTOR INC.; DIRECTOR OF SEVERAL
PROMINENT NORTH-AMERICAN COMPANIES

"*Stewards of the Future: A Guide for Competent Boards* answers the fundamental question facing every board of directors: in our current dynamic environment, what should the board do and what should the board continue to do? This is a must-read treatise that is not just for board chairs but for every director of every corporation, whether public or private, big or small, profit or not-for-profit. I have been involved in the corporate sector in various capacities for my entire career and I gleaned new principles and guidelines for best practice that I had never previously considered by studying *Stewards of the Future*."

PETER DEY,
CHAIR, PARADIGM CAPITAL AND FORMER CHAIR
OF THE ONTARIO SECURITIES COMMISSION

"We live in changing and challenging times, and this puts extra pressure on board members, investors, and executives. What was right yesterday might not be tomorrow. Helle has so much valuable insight and experience, and a unique ability to look into the future and see the next best practices."

JOHN MANLEY, P.C., O.C.,
CHAIR, CAE; DIRECTOR, TELUS; FORMER CEO,
BUSINESS COUNCIL OF CANADA

"Competent boards are key to good corporate governance. Helle Bank Jorgensen has produced a practical and complete reference for boards on how to improve their competence by providing relevant case studies, guidelines, and key questions. Particularly impressive is the insistence on not being satisfied with legal compliance but how board responsibility continues to widen and grow to embrace stewardship for the future."

JERMYN BROOKS,
FORMER CHAIR, BUSINESS ADVISORY BOARD,
TRANSPARENCY INTERNATIONAL

"Good stewardship today requires clear climate and sustainability strategies ... integrated sustainability reporting matters!"

JANE DIPLOCK,
CHAIR, ABU DHABI GLOBAL MARKET REGULATORY COMMITTEE; DIRECTOR, VALUE REPORTING FOUNDATION; DIRECTOR, SINGAPORE EXCHANGE (SGX)

"Boards today will have to navigate the most disruptive future for decades. To do so they will need much more diversity of background and thought and to acquire new skills in systems and futures thinking. *Stewards of the Future* is the guidebook we've been waiting for!"

NIGEL TOPPING,
UN HIGH LEVEL CLIMATE ACTION CHAMPION, COP26

"Tomorrow's most innovative companies will leverage ESG, diversity, and technology to succeed in a changing and ambiguous world. *Stewards of the Future* offers board members a practical guide to lead them on their path."

OLIVIER SCHWAB,
MANAGING DIRECTOR, HEAD OF TECHNOLOGY,
WORLD ECONOMIC FORUM

Climate Change, ESG, Diversity, Human Rights,
Anti-Corruption, Data & Cybersecurity, SDGs, Tax,
Investment, and Pay: Advice from Top Experts

STEWARDS OF THE FUTURE

A GUIDE FOR COMPETENT BOARDS

HELLE BANK JORGENSEN

BARLOW BOOKS
fine books for enterprising authors

Library and Archives Canada Cataloguing in Publication data available upon request.

978-1-988025-76-6 (hardcover)

Printed in Canada

Publisher: Sarah Scott
Book producer: Tracy Bordian/At Large Editorial Services
Cover design: Paul Hodgson
Interior design and layout: Ruth Dwight
Copy editing: Eleanor Gasparik
Proofreading: Joel Gladstone
Indexing: Karen Hunter

For more information, visit **www.barlowbooks.com**

Barlow Book Publishing Inc.,
96 Elm Avenue, Toronto, ON
M4W 1P2 Canada

*For board members everywhere with the
competence, confidence, and courage
to be Stewards of the Future*

Contents

Contents

Thank You...

This book could not have been written without the help and support of so many.

Let me start with the person who helped me get the words on paper, Bernard Simon, a former Canada correspondent for the *Financial Times* and deputy editor of *Business Day* in Johannesburg. When I was introduced to Bernard, he showed me a phone message he had kept from his time at *Business Day*, asking him to call Nelson Mandela. It turned out that the great man had not received his copy of the newspaper that morning. I was sold by the mention of Mandela, a leader I wish I could have met. I hope readers will agree that Bernard has been able to express my thoughts far more eloquently than I could have as a non-native English speaker. It has been such a pleasure working with him.

Besides insights from my own career spanning more than thirty years, this book includes thoughtful quotes and ideas from many global leaders whom I have had the privilege to work with, inspire, and be inspired by over the years. Thank you all for your support of Competent Boards, the training organization I started to bring greater awareness of ESG and sustainability issues to boardrooms. All the leaders mentioned in this book are part of our faculty, willing to share their expertise with board members and executives around the world aiming to complete the Global ESG Competent

Boards Certificate and Designation Program and gain the designation GCB.D. If the book has one shortcoming, it's that I wish we could have included many more of your insights. Alas, space constraints and deadlines forced tough choices. Details of the full faculty and their impressive bios can be found at **www.competentboards.com**.

This book would also not have been possible without the support of my Team Incredible. Thank you to Amy Geisberger, who joined me when Competent Boards was in its infancy and was with me in Davos when we kickstarted the #CompetentBoardsMovement during the 2019 World Economic Forum. Also to Julie Foster, Paa Boateng, Mara Di Loreto, Martina Filipic, Alyssa Merendino, Lena Onupko, Nancy Wright, Elvin Madamba, Pelle Noren, Anabel Labastida, and Jonathan Serravalle—as well as others—who have worked with us and supported us over the years. And a warm thank you to the global leaders who in 2018 supported my idea of offering ESG (environmental, social, and governance) training to board members, among them, Michael Treschow, Paul Polman, Torben Möger Pedersen, Jim Hagemann Snabe, Erika Karp, and Annette Verschuren. Our faculty has now grown to over one hundred world-renowned leaders.

I'm also grateful to all the wonderful "students"—board members, executives, and investors from all over the world—who have joined us to earn the Global Competent Boards Designation (GCB.D). Each week I have the pleasure of learning from about seventy global leaders who join our various programs. Hopefully they also learn a little from me, and the prominent leaders on our faculty, as we share our experiences working with many of the world's finest companies.

I'd like to acknowledge and thank those who inspired me to start this journey. It all began in 1990 with an interview in a local Danish newspaper: Professor Leo Alting of the Danish Technical University spoke about lifecycle analysis, and the amount of water, energy, and waste we could save if the design process was based on lifecycle assessments. I had just completed my business law degree and was studying for a Master of Science in Business Economics and Auditing. I was trying to figure out what my thesis should be about—and there it was in the local newspaper: how to price environmental externalities and embed them into the price of products, and into companies' financial statements.

Leo Alting and his team taught me about lifecycle analysis, and I added the concept of lifecycle and externality costs. Prof. Alting also introduced me to the Danish Steel Works, which recycled steel and wanted to detail its impact on the environment. I was privileged to help the Danish Steel Works develop the world's first "green" account, which was embedded into its 1991 annual financial report.

Another leader to whom I owe much is the late Rob Gray. It was a big day in 1993 when Prof. Gray, then at the University of Dundee in Scotland, included the Danish Steel Works green account in his book *Accounting for the Environment*. I had received a grant to study at the University of Dundee and was so grateful for the insights that Prof. Gray and many other academics from around the world shared with me. I have since learned that Prof. Gray had a similar impact on the careers of many others. I just wish that he could have witnessed the huge strides that the accounting profession has made since he passed away.

I would also like to thank Prof. John Christensen at the University of Southern Denmark in Odense, who marked my thesis *An Informative and True and Fair View of Environmental Reporting*. Both he and the external examiner took the view that my predictions (that we in the future would see externalities embedded in financial reporting) were very interesting but would never happen.

That critique set me on a mission to make it happen, a mission that has defined my career. I truly believe that we manage what we measure and that, unfortunately, we take better care of more expensive resources than free resources, which is why we have seen so much pollution and human suffering as a cost of business. If these externalities had been priced and embedded earlier into financial statements, I'm convinced that we would have seen far more and far quicker innovation in production methods more respectful of our environment, biodiversity, and people.

However, back in the early 1990s, environmental consciousness was not included in any textbook for accountants, nor for that matter, any other profession. It was dismissed as the talk of tree huggers and others who couldn't understand that the business of business was business, in other words, to make as much money as possible without concern for the environmental or social impact, as preached by Milton Friedman in the 1970s. In that climate, it was a miracle that Price Waterhouse hired me in 1992. Full credit goes to Harald Birkwald, hiring partner at Price Waterhouse in Denmark, who, for some reason, was willing to listen to my far-fetched ideas on how important it was for accountants to embed environmental considerations into corporate valuations.

Not long after I joined Price Waterhouse and much to my colleagues' surprise, one of the partners, the late Jørgen Cramon, gave me permission to use 50 percent of my time to build an environmental practice—on the condition that I promised to study hard to become a state-authorized public accountant, a status difficult to attain in Denmark because it gives you the right to sign off on financial statements. I accepted the challenge, and decided that I wanted to sign not only financial accounts but also integrated accounts, which showed both the financial and environmental impact of companies' activities. Needless to say, this made me a rather different kind of accountant from the norm. My questions often resulted in a few moments of silence from clients, followed by a reaction along the lines of: "I don't know, I've never thought about that before." That no doubt made life more difficult for many of my superiors.

Therefore, a warm thank you to all who believed in and all who challenged me. It was a challenge and also a privilege to build and grow the practice, but worth every minute as more and more fantastic colleagues joined the bandwagon.

In 1996, Jermyn Brooks, a partner in our London office, invited me to come and see him. Little did I realize that Jermyn was not "just a partner," but the firm's European leader. A Danish colleague told me that most partners would have given their right arm to meet him, and yet here I was, a young accountant with the title of manager, being summoned to London. On the same visit, I was introduced to many other partners and their work focus, including Glen Peters, who headed the reputation assurance project; David Phillips and his value-reporting project; and Randy Rankin and his responsible supply-chain project. I was drinking from a firehose but felt that the various projects needed to be seen as parts of a whole. I was thrilled when, a few years later, I managed to persuade David Phillips and Prof. Robert Eccles, then at Harvard Business School, that the value-reporting framework also should measure environmental, social, and ethical aspects of a business.

That initial visit to London was followed by discussions with visionary global partners who paved the way to many other opportunities. I got to work with LEGO and IKEA and many other companies on responsible supply-chain programs. While I borrowed insights from my global colleagues, I also integrated environmental, health, and safety considerations into the typical "age, wage, and hours" paradigm that was part of any discussion of sweatshops. I travelled the world with IKEA and trained not only its suppliers but also its procurement and local managers on integrated responsible supply-chain practices. I was fortunate to work with a fantastic team that included Marianne Barner, then a director of IKEA. I was also able to apply my value-reporting insights at Novozymes to create the world's first integrated report, working alongside Anne-Marie Skov, then a vice-president at Novozymes.

I worked with many companies on sustainability reports and strategies, among them, DONG Energy (now Ørsted), Maersk, Novo Nordisk, Royal Dutch Shell, Unilever, and Vestas. And after I passed the state-authorized public accountant exam, I got to sign the assurance statement on the world's first integrated report, issued by Novozymes. A big milestone!

I was named a partner of PwC Denmark in 2000 and, a few years later, was fortunate to join a small group of "young and promising partners" invited to a global strategy meeting.

Each of us was asked to come up with ideas for new practices. Naturally, I suggested that sustainability, environmental, and social considerations should be embedded into all of PwC's offerings. Sam DiPiazza, then PwC's global CEO, as well as the rest of the global leadership team were in the room, and they offered me the opportunity to move to New York to help build and lead the firm's sustainability and climate change practice. I owe Sam and the global leadership team a huge thank you for creating the opportunity to work with other leading global firms, including Nike, to embed sustainability into all their corporate functions.

Before moving to the United States and ahead of the climate negotiations in Copenhagen in 2009, I worked with another leader who has inspired me over the years: Erik Rasmussen, founder of the Danish think-tank Mandag Morgen. At a dinner, Erik seated me at a table with the newly appointed CEO of Unilever, Paul Polman. So began a long conversation, as I had a laundry list of suggestions for what Unilever could and should be doing. Since then, I have had the pleasure of many more discussions with Paul and with the former chair of Unilever Michael Treschow, both of them enthusiastic supporters of Competent Boards.

During my nineteen years with PwC, I was privileged to work with many wonderful colleagues, so many that I can't name them all here. Every one of you has made an impact and has helped me on my way. Also, a warm thank you to the amazing people that I have met since I arrived in Canada in 2012. I have learned so much and have had the chance to meet even more global leaders, including the United Nations Global Compact family as I launched the Compact's Canadian chapter.

This book would not have seen the light of day without the persistence of Sarah Scott, publisher of Barlow Books, who kept pushing me to get it written. Sarah's team, especially Tracy Bordian and Eleanor Gasparik, have been an enormous help in bridging the gulf between writing and printing. A special shout-out to Eleanor for her superb copy-editing.

Beside me all the way has been my dear husband, Jesper Bank Jorgensen. I'm so grateful for the support I have from him and from my daughter Sebrina (who painted the beautiful piece of art that forms the backdrop for the video interviews on which much of this book is based). And of course, my mom, who has taught me so much and given me the strength to say what I mean and the confidence to work on what I love to do. She had to leave school after seventh grade—like so many other women in Denmark and worldwide. She always reminded me to value all the opportunities that others introduced me to.

Thank you to all my dear friends around the world who continue to inspire me.

Finally, I express my gratitude to be living as an uninvited guest on the traditional territories of the Haudenosaunee Confederacy and the Anishinabek Nation. There is no doubt that Indigenous leaders can teach us a lot about stewardship through the ancient Haudenosaunee Seventh Generation Principle, namely, that the decisions we make today should keep the world in a sustainable state seven generations from now.

The Competent Boards Story ...
and Why It Matters

I have had the good fortune to work with many fine companies during my thirty-year career, helping to embed integrated thinking and sustainability in their DNA. Yet all too often, I have come across a big stumbling block: the board of directors has shown little interest in the project. And without the board on board, an *ESG* (environment, social, and governance) project remains just that—an interminable project, and sometimes no more than a pet interminable project.

Another common weakness has been the tendency of boards to fill their ranks with members from similar backgrounds—schools, universities, careers, and business and social networks. Most of them also happen to use the same bathroom. Pale, male boards are also often said to be stale boards, finding it difficult to mesh their own experience with those of others from different walks of life to create a comprehensive view of their company's business and its impact on society. Members of these single-dimension boards tend to focus more on compliance than on innovation and strategy. Worse, some are simply complacent, pleased just to have the title of director and enjoy their pre-meeting dinners.

What if they turned themselves into stewards of the future, determined to assure the long-term success of the company and the communities it touches?

I believe that board members are the most powerful players in a company. They not only hire and fire the CEO but are also the guardians of the company's long-term success. That means agreeing on the purpose of the business, setting the strategic direction, and making informed decisions about what is best for the company and its stakeholders. It certainly means looking after the interests of shareholders, but the responsibility does not stop there. As the founder of India's Tata Group Jamsetji Tata noted more than a century ago: "In a free enterprise, the community is not just another stakeholder in business, but is, in fact, the very purpose of its existence." Much the same thinking drove the founders of the Unilever consumer goods empire (originally Lever Brothers).

In my opinion, the reason many board members do not fulfil these responsibilities is that they operate with less than adequate knowledge of the consequences of their decisions on the broader community. For decades, boards have taken most decisions based only on short-term financial results rather than on long-term costs (as well as benefits) associated with a broader perspective. Figure I.1, from *The Limits to Growth*, vividly illustrates the trajectory that this mindset has put our planet on: more pollution, fewer natural resources, a steady decline in food supplies and industrial output, and—ultimately—a steep rise in deaths.[1] And that chart was published half a century ago, in 1972.

Fifteen years after *The Limits to Growth* was published, the World Commission on Environment and Development, led by former Norwegian prime minister Gro Harlem Brundtland, catalogued the disasters that unfolded in the 900 days between the time that her commission started work in 1984 and publication of its seminal report in 1987. A drought-triggered crisis in Africa had killed as many as a million people. A leak from a pesticides factory in Bhopal, India, killed more than 2,000, and blinded and injured over 200,000 more. Chemicals, solvents, and mercury flowed into the Rhine River during a warehouse fire in Switzerland, killing millions of fish and threatening drinking water supplies in Germany and the Netherlands. The explosion at the Chernobyl nuclear reactor in Ukraine sent nuclear fallout throughout Europe.

FIGURE I.1

Base scenario from *The Limits to Growth* (1972), printed using today's graphics.

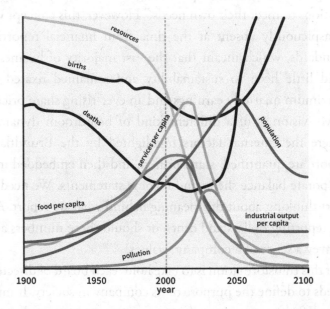

Source: Charles Hall and John Day, "Revisiting the Limits to Growth After Peak Oil," American Scientist 97 (May/June 2009), www.esf.edu/efb/hall/2009-05Hall0327.pdf.

The Chernobyl meltdown made an especially strong impression on me. I was in the United States on a sabbatical after high school at the time, and the catastrophe made me realize that even as we build longer pipelines and higher smokestacks and put local regulations in place to control them, clouds of radioactive pollution do not respect national frontiers. Whether we like it or not, we 7.7 billion humans (as of mid-2021) live in a closed loop, or what some have called a spaceship economy. Chernobyl drove home to me the urgency of changing the way we do business and, in hindsight, helped persuade me to make this my life's work.

The Brundtland report contained this wise definition: "Sustainable development is development that meets the need of the present without compromising the ability of future generations to meet their own needs." However, this concept was conspicuously absent at the time from financial reporting standards, which meant that the vast majority of businesses paid little heed to sustainability and remained fixated on maximum quarterly earnings and an ever-rising share price.

My vision is of a different kind of boardroom dynamic, where the external factors highlighted by the Brundtland report are quantified, standardized, and then embedded into corporate balance sheets and income statements. We need to start thinking about the meaning behind what we report. Are we reporting dollars and cents, or should those numbers also convey a sense of a company's values?

If this transformation is to take hold, each board of directors needs to define the purpose of its company in society. It must also define its own purpose or, to put it another way, how its members will carry out their responsibility as stewards of the company's future. To me, stewardship is about much more than taking care of the resources under a company's ownership. It also requires directors to consider the impact that their actions (or lack of action) will have on the earth's land, its water, its biodiversity, and the health and safety of people beyond the "factory gate."

So what does it take for a member of a corporate board to become a steward of the future?

Start off by asking yourself: What is the purpose of my work? What would my children and grandchildren expect? In other words, am I looking to the future or simply clinging to the past? This book aims to provide some of the answers to those questions and guide readers towards becoming Stewards of the Future.

It is based on my own experience as well as hundreds of interviews and insights that we share with participants in the ESG Competent Boards Certificate and Designation Program. The program was launched during the World Economic Forum in Davos in 2019. Julie Gebauer, global head of human capital and benefits at Willis Towers Watson, kindly allowed us to use her firm's meeting facilities to host a small roundtable discussion so we could launch the #CompetentBoardsMovement in collaboration with Jessica Fries, executive chair of The Prince's Accounting for Sustainability Project (A4S). We also had support from now-retired Unilever chief executive Paul Polman, former Ericsson and Unilever chair Michael Treschow, PensionDanmark CEO Torben Möger Pedersen, and Jim Hagemann Snabe, chair of Siemens and Maersk, as well as from Nik Gowing, a well-known face in Davos as the main presenter for BBC World News for many years.

Despite this impressive backing, many others questioned why ESG should be on any board agenda. We realized that we still had a good deal of work to do before our online training program for corporate directors and other business professionals would win wide acceptance.

I went to see numerous top providers of director education courses and offered our program to them, but was told time and again that directors had no interest in ESG. That was in 2019, and I questioned myself as much as others questioned me about the need for boards of directors to learn the ABCs of ESG. But I persevered. I placed ads in Financial Times Agenda, and I cherished every person who signed up for the ESG Competent Boards Certificate and Designation Program.

Now, two years later, I read in the Financial Times Agenda that the highest priority for board nominating and governance committees is to find candidates who can help guide oversight of ESG issues. The number of board directors and executives taking the Competent Boards program is growing exponentially, and I'm heartened by the fantastic feedback we receive, affirming the program's value and positive impact.

At the heart of the Competent Boards programs is the need for enlightened corporate governance. That can only happen under the stewardship of well-informed board members who can make well-informed decisions. We have begun to see some encouraging results. More and more boards have set up a committee dedicated to wider issues, whether it is called the ESG committee, or the sustainability committee, or something else.

But there is also much work to be done. The 2020 Sustainability Board Report indicated that only 17 percent of board members serving on committees overseeing ESG for the one hundred largest global public companies had the necessary skills to discuss and decide on issues like climate change, cybersecurity, and human rights—three of the most serious risks facing almost every business on earth.[2] How would you, as a board member, feel if only 17 percent of the members of your audit committee could read a profit and loss statement or a balance sheet? Is it any surprise then that activists have taken to accusing companies of "greenwashing" and "green-wishing" when members of a committee overseeing ESG and sustainability are unable to understand the basic ABCs of ESG?

One of our objectives at Competent Boards is to help directors stop greenwashing and green-wishing, and instead do more green-walking, which means more education. I'm grateful to the many directors who have told us that the ESG Competent Boards Certificate and Designation Program has given them the insight and confidence to make well-informed decisions. As Curtis Ravenel, a senior adviser to the COP26 climate conference, recently put it to me: if the directors of ExxonMobil had enrolled in the Competent Boards program, fewer of them might have found themselves tossed out by disgruntled shareholders in the spring of 2021.

It is true that various training programs are available for aspiring and existing corporate directors. But most are based on the premise that a director's role is to maximize value for shareholders—in other words, the company's owners.

What is wrong with that, you might ask? Not much, so long as the directors don't make decisions that "steal" value from others. Unfortunately, existing corporate valuation and accounting systems do not take external costs and benefits into account until an issue hurts the financials and the company's reputation.

I would argue that shareholders, not to mention other stakeholders, gain far more value if the company applies a broader and more proactive mindset. It is clear from this book that many of the world's most respected corporate directors, governance experts, and advisers happen to agree. Once you have read *Stewards of the Future*, I hope that you will, too.

CHAPTER 1

Directors' Dilemmas

"We have to get used to managing under much more uncertainty than we are used to. It's no excuse to say: 'Well, there's too much uncertainty to make decisions.' You are on the board to make decisions, and to move the company on."

–Vagn Sørensen, chair of Air Canada and director of Royal Caribbean Cruises

WHY THIS MATTERS

Corporate boards must navigate a far more complex and challenging landscape today than they did just a few years ago. The combination of globalization, climate change, social activism, and consumer awareness is thrusting threats and opportunities onto boardroom agendas that would have been dismissed not long ago as having little relevance to business. For many companies, new skills, fresh mindsets, and a different culture will be needed to confront this perilous, but also promising, new era.

The *Financial Times* (FT) US business editor Andrew Edgecliffe-Johnson did not mince words when he outlined the challenges in a June 2021 article. "Today's business leaders," Edgecliffe-Johnson wrote, "are being confronted by a new generation of agitators whose aims they consider unrealistic, whose methods they consider unreasonable but whose message will probably prove worth heeding in the long run … From street style to fashions on Wall Street, new ideas tend to start on the fringes."[3] While absolutely correct, the FT article captures only part of the rapid and far-reaching changes that corporate boards currently face. Besides the new generation of players that Edgecliffe-Johnson refers to, board members are also being forced to navigate a myriad of unfamiliar risks and opportunities.

The new generation of "agitators" ranges from environmental activists concerned about climate change and deforestation, to workers pressing for higher minimum wages, social-media influencers, and non-governmental organizations dedicated to stamping out slavery and human trafficking. Equally important is that mainstream investors have joined the calls for companies to pay closer attention to environmental, social, and governance issues, commonly known as ESG. The *Financial Times* reported in July 2021 that funds managing a mammoth US$43 trillion in assets, equal to almost half the world's total, have pledged to meet net-zero carbon emission targets.[4] Indeed, climate, an issue all but ignored by corporate boards at the start of the millennium, is now high on boardroom agendas in almost every industry. Much the same applies to cybersecurity, artificial intelligence, and new movements demanding a variety of social reforms. Most recently, the COVID-19 pandemic has raised a host of new safety and physical and mental health concerns, not to mention the consequences of supply-chain disruptions and new patterns of work.

No issue can be looked at in isolation. Even companies looking to supply, produce, or use solar panels, batteries, or other products essential for reaching a net-zero carbon future must address environmental and social concerns. The batteries may be more carbon-friendly than other forms of power, but mining the metals needed to produce them may cause harm to humans and nature in countries with outdated environmental and human rights laws or lax enforcement.

In the United States, businesses have come under mounting pressure to take a stand on "woke culture," or issues related to social and racial justice, notably the Black Lives Matter movement since the murder of George Floyd in Minneapolis in May 2020. Many businesses have said they will no longer contribute to the campaigns of members of Congress who sought to overturn the results of the November 2020 presidential election. Similarly, companies such as Delta Air Lines and Coca-Cola have distanced themselves from moves to tighten voting rules for future elections. Immigration has emerged as another politically fraught issue that companies are being forced to face head-on, especially those that employ large numbers of migrants. Jan Jones Blackhurst, a former Las Vegas mayor and director of Caesars Entertainment, tells how Caesars began offering domestic partner benefits and lobbied for gay marriage and immigration reform. "We wanted to make a statement that showed our communities and our employees that we were with them, and that we cared about them," Blackhurst notes.

Examining where a company's interests lie on these issues and then taking a stand on them undoubtedly entails time-consuming deliberation and wrenching decisions. But a board shies away from them at its peril. Today's fast-moving environment means that closing our eyes to the world around us and keeping our heads down can no longer be a board's default position. Far better to face unfamiliar threats—and opportunities—directly, and then find fresh ways of confronting them.

Nik Gowing, a former British TV journalist who founded Thinking the Unthinkable, a project aimed at nurturing leaders who thrive on change, has some blunt advice for directors:

> The best thing to do if you can't cope with this is to get out and give the job to somebody who's hungry and prepared to be more humble and more willing to take risks, including the risk of being fired. A good board should be saying to those at the top: "We empower you to take risk to experiment safely. Not to fail safely, but to experiment safely. And we will back you."

HOW TO PREPARE

I discuss below some of the key dilemmas facing boards in the years ahead, as well as ways to navigate them.

Think the Unthinkable

Given the dangerous and unpredictable world we live in, every business now needs to consider the possibility of catastrophic disruptions, and how to survive them. The pandemic has taught some valuable lessons, given that most of us did not see it coming, nor realized the extent to which it would disrupt business and everyday life. COVID's economic and human toll is, albeit belatedly, forcing boards to ask questions like: How do we prepare for future blind spots? How do we plan for resilience in the short-, medium-, and long-term future? How do we plan for and handle risk, and make our scenario planning more robust? What will we do if our market disappears overnight, as happened in the hospitality sector when the pandemic hit? And finally, how can we rethink our business strategy for a zero-carbon future?

Think Like an Activist

If the pandemic has taught anything, it is the importance of taking broad social trends into account when considering potential risks to a business. Board members assumed for many years that shareholder activists and special-interest advocacy groups inhabited another world, and that they would simply have to tolerate discussion of a climate-change or social-justice proposal at the annual meeting. However, attitudes and expectations have changed, especially among employees and consumers younger than the baby boomers who still call most of the shots around boardroom tables. Activism has now reached the boardroom, and it will not be going away any time soon. Analysis of a company's stakeholders—not only its shareholders—and mapping the interaction between critical strategic and financial levers are now essential steps towards ensuring future resilience. However, such exercises should not be confined to avoiding risks. They can also identify opportunities, and the best way to seize them.

Ensure Future Resilience

Today's board should be nudging management towards overhauling supply chains ahead of the competition. Many resources are expected to be in short supply due to climate change and rising living standards, so those plans should include measures to secure commodities that the company may need in the future in a socially and environmentally responsible way. By not looking ahead, a company risks forfeiting the loyalty of suppliers, customers, employees, and many investors. All these stakeholders are looking to the businesses they deal with to offer the consistency, stewardship, accountability, and incentives that will ensure their future well-being even in the most uncertain of circumstances.

Ensure Risk-Management Systems Capture ESG Risks

Given the many uncertainties in the world around us, it is hardly surprising that business risks are proliferating, no matter what sector a company operates in. Any company dependent on external supply chains—and that means most companies on earth—needs to take account of an array of new laws and regulations. It must also keep an eye on emerging social and political trends by monitoring the media, including social media, as well as the communications of its business partners, peers, and rivals. While day-to-day monitoring is not the board's job, board members do need to keep watch for emerging risks and opportunities that can make or break the company's future. Directors should demand that board materials not only capture these developments but also spell out how management plans to deal with them. They should also insist that management provide regular updates and keep abreast of stakeholders' ever-rising expectations.

Agree on Boardroom Responsibilities

The pandemic has underscored the importance of allowing management to get on with its job of running the company without board interference or onerous reporting requirements, even when the unthinkable strikes. Similarly, the experience of the past few years has shown the value of board committees, where experts can thrash out a particular issue and come back to the full board with a recommendation. The very need for more committees may have the side benefit of bringing a wider diversity of skills and backgrounds to the board. But all board members need to understand and act on their stewardship responsibilities.

Jan Jones Blackhurst confirms which way the wind is blowing:

> In the past, audit was probably the most important committee followed by compensation. Today, governance may be one of the most important committees. Boards have to understand how investors are going to be looking at their organizations. They're going to want to know that you're moving towards an inclusive culture. They're going to want to know that you've got minority and gender representation across the board and at all levels of the organization. They want to be comfortable that you're responsibly managing your sustainability practices, that you're very aware of what proper corporate governance is, and that it's not just about shareholder value. It's about building a sustainable organization that not only makes money but also gives back to the communities and the workforce. And that's a very different perspective than has been held by many board members in the past.

Much the same applies to discussions around the boardroom table at Export Development Canada, says the agency's president and CEO Mairead Lavery:

The dialogue has fundamentally shifted. We spend most of our time today talking about non-credit rather than credit risks. Environmental issues, business integrity, how is business actually being conducted, and human rights—these are the issues that we talk to the board about today. And therefore, these are the issues that we're assessing our clients on.

The bottom line is that competent boards will be those emboldened by change, not intimidated by it. Or as Paul Dickinson, co-founder and chair of CDP, which runs a global environmental reporting system backed by almost 600 investors managing US$110 trillion in assets, puts it: "The business leaders who accept the future rather than deny it are the ones who are going to win."

A crisis such as the pandemic reinforces the message that a competent board is also a courageous board. A director's job is to search for the truth, no matter how inconvenient, embarrassing, or costly it may be, and then present it to fellow board members and, if necessary, to management. Boards could take a leaf from the advice that some North American public transit systems drum into their riders: *If you see something, say something.*

Cement the Right Culture

A company's culture should be all-encompassing, from the way people talk to each other at work, to how they view their jobs and their ethical responsibilities. The culture speaks volumes about the company's values and plays a huge role in winning the respect of employees, customers, suppliers, and industry peers. It certainly extends far beyond celebrating the latest quarter's financial results, or a fixation on next year's share price. Indeed, if the culture is right, the financial results and the share price should largely take care of themselves. Conversely, a misguided culture all too often lands a company in serious difficulty. A classic example is Volkswagen (VW), where a disinclination on the part of the board and management to ask tough questions about diesel emissions led to the 2015 scandal that almost brought the German carmaker to its knees. VW said in March 2020 that the diesel scandal had cost it 31.3 billion euros in fines and settlements, and that it expected cash outflows to continue for another year. It agreed three months later to settle claims against four former executives, allowing it to receive 288 million euros in compensation under its directors and officers insurance. Nonetheless, as of mid-2021, VW and its main shareholder Porsche SE were still the target of shareholder claims totalling 4.1 billion euros related to the scandal.[5]

An organization's culture is set at the top, making it one of the board's most critical tasks. Putting the right culture in place starts with hiring the right chief executive. One key yardstick of success, no matter how big the company or in what sector it operates, is whether that culture nurtures resilience, in other words, encourages the board and senior management to keep their gaze on threats and opportunities beyond the current quarter's financial performance.

Another crucial step, according to former Royal Dutch Shell and Bank of America chair Chad Holliday, is to identify relevant "totems" and "taboos"—the former being the qualities most valuable to the company; the latter, the practices considered out of bounds and always discouraged. One of the best ways of articulating totems and taboos, Holliday has found, is to tell specific stories—preferably involving the company itself and its people—that encapsulate the attitudes and behaviours the board is seeking to instill. Positive stories tend to have more impact than negative ones, and the message carries more resonance when the story is told by the CEO or some other senior manager about a junior employee. As an example, Holliday cites his time at Bank of America when senior management spread the word about a customer with a disability who asked a branch manager for help after he was unable to withdraw cash from one of the bank's ATMs. The manager didn't hesitate—she even used her personal credit card to pay for the man's oxygen and overnight accommodation.

A subtle shift in the influence of various board committees is evidence of the growing importance of setting the right corporate culture. The audit and compensation committees have long been accustomed to ruling the roost with their focus on financial results. These days, however, the governance committee often takes the lead in board deliberations, and roughly one in ten S&P 500 boards now have committees focused on environmental, social, and governance issues.[6] Changes such as these can send a powerful message that the board and top management are intent on moving towards a more inclusive culture based on more than shareholder value. The message should be directed at building a sustainable organization, where giving back to the community and the workforce is an embedded part of value creation. It is about making money in a sustainable and responsible manner, not about how the money is spent.

Instilling a more inclusive culture may require some major changes at board level. Silos need to be broken down, which means appointing more directors who are skilled in inter-disciplinary approaches and are effective communicators, especially in conveying bad news. Many boards and senior managers try to paper over or even ignore tough issues, but that approach is finding less favour as pressure grows for honesty and transparency, especially in times of crisis. Board members need to learn to disagree respectfully, and then work towards finding common solutions that take into account all stakeholders' priorities.

At the same time, board members should spare no effort to affirm the CEO, senior management, and each other. But they should not shy away from putting in a quiet word when colleagues' behaviour falls short. Chad Holliday recalls that during his time as DuPont's chief executive, one director typically flew in from Europe four or five hours prior to each board meeting. He would spend much of that time with Holliday, coaching and counselling him as they discussed the company's affairs. After one such session, Holliday thanked him profusely for his time and support. As Holliday tells it, the director "leaned back in his chair and said: 'Hey, don't get confused. I back you till I sack you.'"

Recognize a New Meaning of Fiduciary Duty

The vast majority of US board members have long assumed they have a fiduciary duty only to the company's owners, in other words, the shareholders. And that view has found no shortage of support among shareholders themselves, not to mention corporate lawyers.

However, that narrow approach is making way for the view that companies have a wider duty of stewardship that also includes their employees, their customers and suppliers, and society at large. These responsibilities are increasingly being codified in laws, regulations, and codes of conduct. Section 172 of the UK Companies Act, for example, clearly suggests that a company's duty to its shareholders comes after its responsibility to everyone else. More than thirty US states now make provision for "benefit corporations," which are legally bound to consider the impact of their decisions on all stakeholders.[7] What's more, boards and management themselves are coming to realize that what is good for society at large also invariably benefits shareholders. Thus, the backlash against fossil fuels is having a profound impact on consumer preferences, as shown by the rising popularity of electric vehicles and renewable energy. Any company that fails to recognize such trends is surely not acting in the best interests of its shareholders.

The evolving definition of fiduciary duty requires corporate directors to take a longer-term view of the business than most are accustomed to. That involves two important changes in how boards do their job. First, competent boards will pay less attention to next quarter's earnings and share price. Second, they will look for ways to devise an early warning system for events and issues with the potential to harm the firm's finances and reputation.

Figure 1.1, taken from the *Copenhagen Charter*, a document I co-authored in 1999, illustrates the above point. It describes the concept of "stakeholder reporting," a valuable business intelligence tool that helps management respond swiftly to potential opportunities and threats. The inner loop describes how an improved stakeholder information system enables a company to react faster to events in the environment around

FIGURE 1.1

"Early warning" system. Paying attention to stakeholder signals (inner loop) allows management to react to changes in stakeholders' behaviour before the latter impacts the bottom line (outer loop).

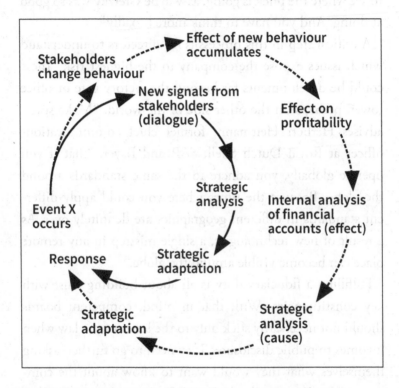

Source: *The Copenhagen Charter,* http://base.socioeco.org/docs /doc-822_en.pdf.

it. If management relies only on traditional financial accounts for its information, as shown in the outer loop, it risks being unaware of changes in stakeholder behaviour until they show up on the bottom line, in other words, until it is too late.[8]

The next chapter describes in more detail several initiatives currently underway to harmonize these measurements in ways that are as easy to understand as reading a balance sheet or a profit and loss account. As Annette Verschuren, a veteran of numerous Canadian boards, puts it, the bottom line for directors is that "you have to understand the future. You have to see where the puck is going, as Wayne Gretzky was so good at doing. And you have to think more broadly."

A critical step in this process is for directors to understand which issues expose the company to the highest risk. These could be developments far beyond the factory gate or office tower, perhaps on the other side of the world. "Make sure," advises Herbert Heitmann, former chief communications officer at Royal Dutch Shell, SAP, and Bayer, "that if you operate globally, you adhere to the same standards around the globe. Because the times where you could apply different standards in different geographies are definitely over. As a result of new technologies, a single misstep in any remote place can become visible around the globe."

Fulfilling a fiduciary duty is all about building trust with key constituencies. With that in mind, competent boards should not necessarily stick only to the letter of the law when it comes to public disclosure. They need to go further, asking themselves what they would want to know about the company if they were in the position of an investor or any other stakeholder. They need to agree on what kind of company they want to be responsible for, and to ensure that their management team has the same vision and values. And then, they must work to build trust with all stakeholders.

"You must seize every opportunity to build trust," says Chad Holliday, "because one instant can destroy it all. So take advantage of all the times you can do it. Especially during this difficult time, we're trying to communicate more frequently, and be sure we're communicating to all investors, not selectively in any way whatsoever." One way that Shell has accomplished that is for the chair and several other board members to meet with investors every two years, and collectively answer their questions. "We got very good feedback from investors that they really understood what we thought and what was going on," Holliday recalls. "They could visualize it as a boardroom because they saw us going back and forth on the stage."

Keep an Eye on Long-Term Goals

There are times, as the pandemic has shown, when a company has little choice but to concentrate on survival. No board or management can ignore poor performance, and a business is sure to wither if it keeps stumbling from quarter to quarter. In navigating sporadic upheavals, however, the board should not be tempted to lower its gaze from the distant horizon, and even beyond.

The hard truth is that a business does not create real value from one quarter to the next. Most companies take at least four or five years to build a solid and sustainable business. In the case of an energy or mining company, it could take even longer. Even an investment in a new information technology system may take several years to pay off. So why are we so focused on quarterly numbers? Swedish business leader Michael Treschow, who once headed Unilever's board, told me years ago that we should focus on how a company manages long-term outcomes based on the right short-term decisions.

A company with a clear vision of its future generally outperforms one that puts short-term results first, and the board has a pivotal role in keeping it on that track. FCLTGlobal, a non-profit research group, has identified several traits common to boards that have their eyes firmly set on the long term. First, they spend more time on strategy. Second, they ensure that directors have a stake in the success of the business, usually by owning a sizable chunk of stock. Third, the faces around the board table reflect the diversity of the society in which the company operates. Finally, the directors make a point of communicating with shareholders directly, and not only through management.

In taking these actions, boards must inevitably make choices that involve trade-offs and dilemmas. Unfortunately, short-run solutions all too often emerge as the preferred course of action. While boards typically appreciate the importance of thinking and acting for the long term, they are also under constant pressure to fight the fires burning around them. According to McKinsey & Company and FCLTGlobal, 70 percent of directors and CEOs would take actions that do not enhance long-term goals so they can meet short-term financial targets.[9] Ironically, almost half of corporate executives point to their boards as unexpected sources of short-term pressure, impeding long-term strategic thinking.[10]

The pandemic has, if anything, exacerbated this problem. Six out of every ten CEOs and C-suite executives at European companies told EY that the pandemic had challenged their ability to focus on long-term growth. The same number said that it had sparked significant differences of opinion within leadership teams on how to balance short-term priorities with long-term investments.[11]

There are other dilemmas, too. If a company encourages board members to own more stock, how does it discourage them from becoming preoccupied, like everyone else, with the short-term ups and downs of the stock market? Much as a company may wish to attract a diverse and talented board, it may face intense competition for top-drawer candidates and end up settling for second best. And how should the board communicate directly with shareholders without undermining management or putting out conflicting messages?

FCLTGlobal has several suggestions to help boards set the right priorities. It advises committees to do the heavy lifting on complex issues, then take them to the full board for an informed, high-level conversation and decision. Board members should be sent relevant reading materials in advance so that they come to meetings prepared for discussion and decisions. Time-allocation tools can help analyze how long the board spends on various topics. The temptation for directors to be swayed by short-term movements in the share price can be mitigated by locking up their stock holdings for several years, perhaps even until they leave the board, and beyond. FCLTGlobal also advises a steady turnover of board members to strike a balance between those with the wisdom of experience and others who bring a fresh perspective. Interviews with potential board members should always include questions about their commitment to the company's long-term success. "Directors who are good in crisis and also good in long-term strategy work are hard to find," says Sarah Keohane Williamson, FCLTGlobal's chief executive. "But those are the ones that truly add value over time."

Manage Shareholder Expectations

Even as boards move away from the view that their fiduciary duty is solely to shareholders, those shareholders are becoming ever more demanding. Many are clamouring for greater transparency and more proactive engagement from the board and management. BlackRock, one of the world's largest asset managers, voted against management on one or more proposals at 42 percent of all shareholder meetings between mid-2020 and mid-2021, up from 39 percent the previous year. Corporate governance concerns prompted most of its votes against director nominations.[12] On the other hand, some shareholders—call them speculators if you like—are looking for a quick bonanza rather than a long-term strategy. The abundance of liquidity in capital markets in recent years and pressure for higher returns in an environment of rock-bottom interest rates have given these shareholders enormous power at a time when boards need to consider other constituencies as well. The same goes for bondholders who, arguably, wield even more influence, as they can demand changes without having to follow the costly and time-consuming proxy solicitation process typically required for a successful shareholder revolt.

In many cases boards are no longer dealing only with individual shareholders or with institutions acting alone. Increasingly, they are confronted by powerful groups that have similar goals and are coordinating their approaches to the companies they invest in. One such group is EOS, the stewardship service arm of UK-based Federated Hermes, which engages with companies on environmental, social, and governance issues on behalf of institutional investors and bondholders. As of mid-2021, Hermes's clients managed assets totalling US$1.3 trillion, and it employed almost

2,000 people in offices across North America, Europe, and Asia. "Our engagement activities enable long-term institutional investors to be more active owners of their assets," Hermes says on its website. "We believe this is essential to build a global financial system that delivers improved long-term returns for investors, as well as better, more sustainable outcomes for society." Timothy Youmans, North American lead for EOS at Federated Hermes, puts it this way: "There's a difference between active shareholding and activism. Talking to investors is the number one way for boards to inoculate themselves against activism and proxy fights."

One result of this growing clout is that boards must now engage with shareholders not only during proxy season or at the annual general meeting, as was usually the case in the past, but also throughout the year. Indeed, proxy voting has become the last resort for many shareholders who prefer to engage in a constant dialogue with the companies they invest in.

Whether it be the growing interest in environmental, social, and governance issues or the pressure for quick returns, the heat on corporate boards is undoubtedly rising. There can be little doubt, however, as to which side boards need to come down on. As Paul Polman, former Unilever CEO, puts it:

> Only running your company for the short term is not going to do it any more. The average length of a publicly traded company was sixty-seven years when I was born, and has dropped to seventeen years now. So only running your company for the shareholders is devastating. Because ultimately, you'll lose your purpose, you'll lose your focus. While it is easy to optimize your short-term returns and get your short-term share price up, it's very difficult to maintain that.

Instead, the board's highest priority should be to retain and nurture the company's key resources. That may mean cutting the dividend when liquidity is tight, or taking whatever steps are necessary to retain the best people when competitors come knocking on the door.

Directors and managers are all too often hesitant to share their long-term strategies with outsiders, even shareholders, because they fear that even the best-laid plans may be disrupted by shifting market conditions, government policies, and innumerable other uncertainties. However, these fears underestimate savvy investors' willingness to accept the need for flexibility as conditions change, whether it is a sudden surge in interest rates, a new tariff on imports from China, or—who could possibly have predicted?—a savage global pandemic. Shareholders are likely to have less patience with boards that have either no long-term transition strategy or a plan that is so vague and opaque that it is of no value at all.

Some directors still view regular dialogue with shareholders as either unnecessary or undermining of management's authority. Yet FCLTGlobal has found that boards that engage directly with shareholders are better positioned to communicate the company's long-term strategy, especially if the board members are long-term shareholders themselves. Done effectively, this communication can attract a cadre of loyal investors, giving the company a layer of protection against unwelcome activists. Further, it can help ensure that capital markets value the company appropriately—70 to 90 percent of a stock's value is based on projected cash flows three or more years into the future. Managers also acknowledge that communicating with people outside the company has led to better business decisions and to closer alignment with the board. The company secretary can be especially helpful in building these bridges. Usually to be found quietly taking notes at the end of the boardroom table, the secretary has the knowledge and access to resources that can smooth the way for the board to communicate directly with outside shareholders.

Use Incentives to Drive Appropriate Behaviour

Incentives of one kind or another can play a powerful role in driving behaviours, both wanted and unwanted, and, as a result, can be a strong lever in shaping corporate culture. At worst, a company can quickly find itself in troubled waters if unethical behaviour is encouraged, or even tolerated, based on misguided incentives. On the other hand, appropriate incentives can go a long way towards aligning the board and management with the company's long-term goals, including an emphasis on environmental, social, and governance issues.

More and more companies are tying executive remuneration, at least in part, to ESG performance as a way of encouraging managers to take sustainability more seriously. Kevin Coon, an international human rights and labour rights lawyer based in Toronto, cites the example of health and safety regulations in the Canadian province of Ontario. With the province ratcheting up fines for violations, compliance with these rules has become a critical yardstick for evaluating executive performance—and thus compensation. The penalties have reached a level where they can no longer be dismissed as simply a cost of doing business, with the result that attention to health and safety has become a dramatically more important element in corporate culture. "Compensation can drive behaviour," Coon notes, "and if it's positive behaviour you want on issues like sustainability or human rights, you build it into the compensation system in some fashion."

As with all key policies, incentives need to be re-evaluated periodically to ensure short- and long-term value creation. This review process is especially important at this time to take account of developments such as the volatility of financial markets and the extra demands made on management during the pandemic and by the looming climate and bio-diversity crisis. Incentives for rank-and-file employees may also need to be adapted to shifting expectations. For example, incentives for safe practices on the shop floor or at construction sites could help boost workers' morale.

Done right, incentives can help a company navigate turbulent times without resorting to such drastic action as replacing the chief executive or announcing a radical change in direction. They can encourage imaginative thinking and long-term planning. Jim Hagemann Snabe, who chairs the boards of the German electrical engineering group Siemens and Denmark's Maersk shipping line, observes that "you have to lead in a way where you inspire the organization to reinvent itself from a position of strength, and not wait until the company is in trouble." The board has to drive an open outside-in strategy process and define the right measures of success and incentives to make that happen. According to Snabe:

> In times of radical change, you constantly need to challenge the status quo, and question your assumptions. With the technologies available today, we have the biggest

opportunity ever to reinvent business models to become more relevant and sustainable. That's the dream. I always challenge myself: What could I do better for business and society? I think that is the recipe for long-term success and a sustainable future.

The incentives do not need to take the form of bonuses, stock options, or other financial perks. There are many other ways of rewarding stellar performance and, unlike many financial incentives, doing so publicly in a way that the recipients' achievements are widely recognized and become inculcated in the corporate culture. As Chad Holliday puts it: "I think we often miss the emotional side, which is really critical." A sincere thank you and a round of applause can go a long way towards motivating employees at all levels.

CASE STUDY: ROYAL DUTCH SHELL

All directors must deal with tricky dilemmas, but some are trickier than others. That is especially true for board members of high-profile energy producers facing demands to transition to a future of net-zero carbon emissions. As one of the world's top 10 energy producers, Shell takes the view that it should also have a top 10 board. "We decided that if Shell was to make the transition from old forms of energy to new forms of energy, we needed a great board," says Chad Holliday, the company's chair from 2015 to 2021.

Holliday and his colleagues set out to achieve that goal by conducting as much research as possible on how a top 10 board adds value to a company. Among their conclusions were the following:

- The board can never match senior executives' knowledge of the energy industry. What it can bring is a diverse perspective. Almost half of Shell's board members are now women, and its directors come from a variety of nationalities and backgrounds.

- It is important to bring issues to the board well before management makes major decisions. The goal is for the board to have input two or three times along the way and to have enough time to discuss the issue thoroughly. The general guideline has been that if the board sets aside an hour for an agenda item, twenty minutes is spent on the presentation and forty minutes on discussion.

- The board does not have to spend an entire meeting around the same table. Members can break into small groups, perhaps with senior management, and then come back.

- Board members must listen carefully to what management tells them.

Shell has found that it needs to respond much faster than it did a decade ago, whether to investors or environmental activists. The board has played a role in speeding up those responses, mainly by anticipating issues before they appear on management's radar screen, given that management is focused on running the business.

The company has also become increasingly aware of the contribution and influence of young people eager to make an impact on the world, including its own employees. While Holliday was chair, he made a point of having lunch two or three times a month with young employees from across the company. He would ask questions like: Are we moving fast enough? Are we working on the right things? Do you feel encouraged about what you're doing? "That's kind of my barometer for whether we are meeting their needs," he says. "I know that if they don't feel we're making enough progress, we won't keep them. They'll vote with their feet."

Besides the usual board committees, Shell has a committee dedicated to the environment, sustainability, and safety. Its members travel twice a year to communities where the company has operations and make a point of consulting not only the leaders of those communities but also workers and their families. The board also sets up special committees from time to time to deal with specific issues that require extra time and focus.

Holliday says that a critical element in reaching wise decisions is not to shut down a conversation prematurely, but instead to listen. He has coached members of Shell's management to ask follow-up questions and dig a bit deeper, rather than brusquely telling colleagues they are wrong. In a similar vein, when Shell's board reviews a complex project, members are encouraged to set up one-on-one conversations with the relevant expert in management so that they can ask whatever questions they like without feeling they are making fools of themselves in public.

■■■

Guidelines for Competent Boards

» Draw up a statement of the company's long-term purpose that goes beyond feel-good platitudes.

» Agree on who your most material stakeholders are—and why—and how far you will go to satisfy their expectations.

» Acknowledge that you do not know the answer to everything. Listen to colleagues, employees, and outside experts who know more than you do.

» Ask questions, rather than shut down a conversation. Learn to ask more probing questions.

» Encourage respectful disagreement, and make time to hear all viewpoints before coming to decisions.

» Examine the environmental and social risks associated with your business in the short, medium, and long run. Then define the level of risk acceptable to the board, and consider what is acceptable to your stakeholders.

» Put the long term above the short term, no matter how strong the pressures to do otherwise. And make sure that short-term decisions lead to desired long-term goals.

» Make sure stakeholders, and not just shareholders, are aware of the company's long-term plans through regular communication, especially with the chair or lead director.

» Ask "what if?" questions, adopt scenario planning, and revisit the plans regularly. That will help uncover blind spots and avoid being trapped in a failed short-term strategy.

» Use remuneration structures that help management focus on the long-term health of the company. Bear in mind non-financial incentives—even a simple thank you—are an effective way of boosting performance and loyalty.

Ten Key Questions

(Recommended exercise: Ask each director to answer these questions independently. Then compare and discuss. More details on page 231.)

1. How often does your board discuss different scenarios that may impact the business in the future?

2. How often do you discuss whether management has the necessary expertise and resources to respond to a disruptive environment?

3. How do you know if your corporate culture encourages sustainability and the overall purpose you have set for the company?

4. Are you aware of the processes, including controls, needed to promote the corporate culture that the board wishes to promote?

5. Does your board's behaviour reflect the behaviour expected throughout the company?

6. What is your board doing to ensure wise long-term stock ownership among directors?

7. Is your board committed to diversity, equity, and inclusion in its own ranks? Do board members mirror your desired mix of talent and customers, now and in the future? Do you have enough younger people and women as well as first-time directors with fresh perspectives?

8. Does the board talk to investors and key stakeholders throughout the year, or only at the annual meeting and during proxy season?

9. Should your board re-evaluate the amount of time it spends on financial performance versus ESG and behavioural performance and strategy?

10. Does your company curb excessive executive compensation and ensure compensation is equitable at all levels?

Reflections

"The first fossil fuel company that steps forward and says 'we are sunsetting our assets.' The first consumer goods company that says 'we are sunsetting our single-use plastic.' The first large food company that says 'we are sunsetting our use of XYZ chemical fertilizers and insecticides because they are destroying the future.' The first companies that do those things will have the best staff in the world and the best investors in the world, ready to work together."

–*Amy Larkin, author of* Environmental Debt: The Hidden Costs of a Changing Global Economy

CHAPTER 2

Three Letters that Matter

"There will be more scrutiny of ESG by investors, by the SEC, by listing agencies, and by anyone else who has some control or authority over a company."

–Janet Hill, director, Carlyle Group and Esquire Bank

WHY THIS MATTERS

Sustainability ... corporate responsibility ... business purpose ... corporate statesmanship ... social responsibility ... ESG ... Call it what you like, competent boards can no longer afford to put environmental, social, and governance—ESG for short—issues on the back burner. Not long ago, these matters—ranging from freak weather events to demands for a higher minimum wage and the diversity of board members—were widely considered to have no place on a board agenda. Now, however, directors ignore them at their peril—hence this book and the ESG Competent Boards Certificate and Designation Program.

A study by Tensie Whelan, director of the NYU Stern Center for Sustainable Business, reported in early 2021 that very few of the 1,188 Fortune 100 board members surveyed had sufficient ESG experience.[13] While many directors have obtained the ESG Competent Boards Certificate and Designation in recent years, table 2.1 shows that the proportion of those with

TABLE 2.1

ESG credentials among board members.

S Categories	% With Relevant Credentials	E Categories	% With Relevant Credentials	G Categories	% With Relevant Credentials
Workplace diversity	5.0% (60)	Energy	1.2% (14)	Accounting oversight/experts	2.6% (31)
Healthcare (physicians, hospital, clinic boards, etc.)	3.5% (41)	Conservation/ nature	1.2% (14)	Regulatory body (SEC, FCC)	1.0% (12)
Health challenges/ advocacy	1.9% (22)	Sustainable business	.8% (10)	Cyber/telecom security	.6% (8)
CSR/ESG	1.5% (18)	Sustainable development	.8% (10)	Risk	.4% (5)
Civil/human rights	1.5% (18)	Environmental law	.5% (6)	Ethics/corruption/ corporate responsibility	.3% (4)
Youth education, health, safety	1.2% (14)	Environmental protection	.5% (6)	Fiduciary/director responsibility	.3% (4)
Economic / community development	1.1% (13)	ESG investing	.3% (4)	Governance	.1% (2)
Human resources	.8% (10)	Climate	.2% (3)		
Adult education	.7% (9)	Water	.1% (2)		
Nonprofit CEO	.7% (9)				
Philanthropy	.7% (9)				
Sustainable development	.5% (6)				
Media/arts	.3% (4)				
Public policy	.3% (4)				
Affordable housing	.2% (3)				
Workplace benefits	.1% (2)				
Nutrition	.1% (2)				
Workplace safety	.08% (1)				
ESG Investing	.08% (1)				

Source: NYU Stern Centre for Sustainable Business 2021 survey.

relevant ESG credentials remains far too small.[14] Which raises the question: How can we ask board members to oversee and make well-informed decisions on how a company should tackle these pressing issues if so few are familiar with them?

The forces pushing boards to expand their ESG knowledge are gathering momentum. One such noteworthy trend is that pension funds, mutual funds, and other powerful investors are devoting more resources to understanding ESG issues, thereby raising awareness, expertise, and sophistication in this area. They are also asking boards more incisive questions to ensure that they are in line with the mushrooming array of ratings, rankings, benchmarks, and other ways of measuring sound ESG practices.

Any board member tempted to ignore this movement would be well advised to read the proxy voting guidelines drawn up by major asset managers, or just Larry Fink's annual letter to BlackRock shareholders. Fink, BlackRock's founder, chair, and CEO, announced in 2020 that in the future his firm, the world's largest asset manager, would consider sustainability as a core goal in its investment decisions.[15] "Awareness is rapidly changing, and I believe we are on the edge of a fundamental reshaping of finance," Fink wrote. "The evidence on climate risk is compelling investors to reassess core assumptions about modern finance." BlackRock's announcement came only a few months after 180 members of the powerful US Business Roundtable broke with tradition by pledging to serve not only their owners but also workers, customers, suppliers, and communities.[16] The roundtable's original 1997 mission statement declared: "The paramount duty of management and of boards of directors is to the corporation's stockholders." The interests of other stakeholders, like employees or local communities, were only "relevant as a derivative of the duty to stockholders." But from now on, it asserted: "Each of our stakeholders is essential."

In a similar vein, the World Economic Forum revised its Davos Manifesto in late 2019 to recognize that the concept of "shareholder capitalism" had been discredited by pressures on companies to boost their short-term financial results, giving rise to a single-minded focus on profits.[17] Instead, the emphasis in the future would be on "stakeholder capitalism" with a far wider audience. As Klaus Schwab, the forum's founder and executive chair, explained:

> One likely reason is the "Greta Thunberg" effect. The young Swedish climate activist has reminded us that adherence to the current economic system represents a betrayal of future generations, owing to its environmental unsustainability. Another (related) reason is that millennials and Generation Z no longer want to work for, invest in, or buy from companies that lack values beyond maximizing shareholder value. And, finally, executives and investors have started to recognize that their own long-term success is closely linked to that of their customers, employees, and suppliers.

All this is happening at the same time as modern technology is disrupting existing business models, enabling outsiders, whether investors or activists, to shine a brighter light on a company's practices and its transparency in dealing with ESG issues. Georg Kell, founding director of the United Nations Global Compact, notes that with help from social media and other technology, formal authority is eroding, empowering ordinary people around the world in a way that was never possible before. As a result, it has become more difficult for established authorities, including business leaders, to filter their messages or hide information they would prefer outsiders not to know about. Kell sees these developments as "no longer a question of communications or CEO nice talk, or just saying the right thing, but it has become a material, substantive issue for survival and growth."

Thus, employees can no longer be viewed simply as a cost centre that needs to be contained. As business becomes more knowledge intensive, workers are increasingly seen as valuable assets that, like any other, need to be protected and nurtured. As stewards of the future, board members must ensure that policies are geared to that end. The reward will be that the company continues to attract the talent required to fulfill its purpose. Think of it as a social contract where money is just one element. For many employees, continued learning and growth opportunities in a company that they take pride in are as important as a salary in cementing loyalty. The alternative is disgruntled employees venting their unhappiness on social media, Glassdoor, and similar platforms, thereby creating even more problems for their bosses.

As with employees, many ESG components—think also of the goodwill of local communities, strong relationships with investors and regulators, and so on—are basically intangible assets that can markedly influence a company's financial performance and its value. In the eyes of many experts, ESG performance has become a proxy for judging the resilience of a company's overall business strategy. As Aron Cramer, CEO of BSR, a group of sustainable business experts, puts it: "If you're not managing ESG factors well, you're probably not anticipating the changes in the world, or enough of the changes in the world that are going to ultimately determine whether a company's strategy is on the right track or not."

Ignoring or downplaying ESG issues now carries significant risks—financial, legal, and reputational. Take the bankruptcy filing by the California utility PG&E as a result of claims stemming from huge wildfires. PG&E pleaded guilty in mid-2020 to eighty-four counts of involuntary manslaughter, the deadliest US corporate crime ever successfully prosecuted.[18] "These issues should become and are increasingly becoming part of boards' fiduciary duty, even if they're not written in law," says Kell. "Ignoring them could be devastating both for business and society, and getting them right, extremely rewarding."

For board members, such developments may not only cause sleepless nights but also threaten their jobs. Shareholders filed at least 467 ESG-related resolutions—a new record—during the 2021 proxy season, according to *Forbes* magazine.[19] As of early July, shareholders had approved thirty environmental and social proposals at Russell 3000 companies, up 50 percent from the total number passed during the 2020 proxy season.[20] Nowhere was the threat to directors more forcefully on display than at ExxonMobil, where a little-known activist hedge fund, Engine No. 1, won three board seats after demanding that the oil and gas giant take a more assertive stance on climate change.[21] Every board member, no matter in what sector, would do well to study how Engine No. 1 was able to successfully attack one of the world's most powerful corporations.

HOW TO PREPARE

Robert Rubinstein, chair and founding partner of TBLI Group, a Dutch non-profit that helps mobilize money flows into ESG investing, has a pithy but valuable piece of advice for corporate directors when it comes to ESG oversight: "You must be serious, not just curious."

What does "serious, not just curious" mean in practice? In general, investors are looking for focus, clear articulation, consistency, and transparency. Anirban Ghosh, Mahindra's chief sustainability officer, describes how the Indian conglomerate has moved in that direction:

> For the last five or six years, we've been having ESG calls with investors, sharing with them what we are doing, seeking their input and their feedback. It's also about understanding and learning from them what makes sense from their perspective. These calls have evolved. Initially, they were more one-way communication with few questions. Today, there are many more questions, many suggestions. It's not like they are trying to pin you down or ask you very difficult questions. It's far more collegial. It's more like a team; it's almost as if we're trying to solve the same problems together. In recent times, our organization has been called in to talk to investors on how ESG helps drive business numbers. It does drive the numbers well for us. So we have a story to tell.

And the story is being told: "Doing business for good is as important to us as doing good business," Mahindra's website notes.

Expectations for ESG disclosure have ballooned in recent years, and boards need to familiarize themselves with the ever more demanding standards being set by investors and regulators. Among the best places to start: the prototype climate-related financial disclosure standards produced by several sustainability and integrated reporting groups in December 2020 and, as of summer 2021, being refined by the International Financial Reporting Standards (IFRS) Foundation;[22] the US Securities and Exchange Commission's statement on the review of climate-related disclosure;[23] the EU's sustainable finance disclosure regulations, which took effect in March 2021;[24] the requirements for mandatory reporting adopted by several countries as outlined by the Task Force on Climate-related Financial Disclosures (TCFD);[25,26] and BlackRock's now-famous CEO letters. A growing number of long-established financial regulators and standards setters, such as the International Organization of Securities Commissions (IOSCO) and the IFRS Foundation, are making it clear that companies should expect to integrate ESG reporting into traditional financial reporting frameworks and to have this information audited along with the usual financial numbers.

Yet many boards are struggling to meet these expectations. Directors are unsure which of the array of ESG issues deserve their attention. They are unaware of the exact data and format that stakeholders want and hesitate to provide information that has the potential to be misleading or misunderstood. And they are confused by the multitude of ESG guidelines, standards, advisory services, measurement tools, and rankings that have proliferated in recent years. I examine these concerns in greater detail below; however, Anirban Ghosh's advice is simple:

Start with whatever you think is most important for your business. But just get started. If you think ten units of progress is doable, set that as your goal and get started. You will soon discover that it is possible to do one hundred units of good work. Then you can scale up your targets, and enjoy the benefits that accrue to the business, the environment, and society because of concerted climate action.

ESG Disclosure

Many boards are reluctant to set ambitious ESG goals, and even more reticent to communicate those goals beyond the boardroom and executive suite. They fear being held liable, either in a formal legal sense or in the unforgiving court of public opinion. On both counts, however, the risks appear to be diminishing rather than growing. Far from being punished for disclosure, companies are more likely to face blowback, in the form of lawsuits and public hostility, if they fail to disclose enough information on labour practices, energy use, compensation, and any number of other ESG issues. Among the risks: if a company fails to provide adequate information on its ESG activities, firms that compile ESG ratings and rankings will use incomplete or even inaccurate data published online by other parties to fill in the blanks. In short order, the company is likely to find itself on the defensive to investors and ESG advocacy groups. Far better to be proactive and reap the benefits of transparency.

Boards should view ESG disclosure as a two-way street. On one hand, they would be wise to ensure that the company responds as fully as possible to regulatory requirements and investors' requests. But disclosure is also a way to demonstrate commitment and foster dialogue. "If you look at the institutional investor community, they are leveraging the use of engagement to help shape and drive corporate practices and behaviours for long-term value creation," says Bonnie Saynay, ISS ESG's global head of ESG research and data strategy. "Divestment really becomes the only outcome if you find a company that is not willing to be responsive or has not indicated remedial action to rectify any corporate malpractice." Some investors choose to engage directly with companies, while others prefer to work through a specialist organization, such as Federated Hermes, that represents investors' sustainability concerns.

Whatever the undoubted benefits of disclosure, it does carry risks that boards need to take into account. ESG disclosures now face almost the same degree of scrutiny as financial regulatory filings, but without the safety net that insurance policies offer for information vetted by a financial auditor. This means that companies need to be more careful what they measure, how they measure it, and how accurate it is. In other words, ESG disclosures nowadays must meet the same robust standards as financial reports, even though few individuals understand how to collect, test, and present ESG data in the same rigorous format as financial data. Reporting facts and figures for the sake of reporting them, without a well-thought-out purpose and without close scrutiny, is a waste of everyone's time, exposing the company (and the board) to accusations of greenwashing and "impact washing."

The key yardstick for deciding which ESG information to make public is materiality, in other words, whether the information is material to the company's overall strategy and operations or to its stakeholders. Several organizations have drawn up standards aimed at creating a common language to report on ESG issues in a credible and consistent way that meets the needs of investors, policy-makers, capital markets, and civil society. Among the most widely used are those developed by two independent non-profits: Amsterdam-based GRI and the Sustainability Accounting Standards Board (SASB), based in San Francisco, which merged in June 2021 with the International Integrated Reporting Council (IIRC) to form the Value Reporting Foundation. Both seek to identify environmental, social, and governance issues most relevant to different industries. GRI looks at materiality from the perspective of a wide group of stakeholders using thousands of reporters in over one hundred countries to draw up its standards. SASB focuses on financial stakeholders and has drawn up criteria for seventy-seven different sectors. Venetia Bell, chief sustainability officer at London-based GIB Asset Management, which manages US$11 billion, says that, from a governance perspective, the merger of SASB and IIRC "helps integrate thinking across the organization and weaves this conversation around sustainability into the boardroom and effective communication with stakeholders."

The array of standards and frameworks produced by an alphabet soup of non-governmental organizations and regulators is gradually making way for harmonization and collaboration. That is indisputably a step forward, since the many well-meaning reporting initiatives, frameworks, and standards have triggered much confusion, often resulting in a waste of time and resources. One outcome of the convergence is that the IFRS Foundation will oversee the International Sustainability Standards Board (ISSB) as a parallel organization to the International Accounting Standards Board (IASB), which develops and approves international financial reporting standards adopted by over 140 countries.

The IOSCO has encouraged the IFRS Foundation and the ISSB to use existing sustainability-related reporting principles and guidance as building blocks for investor-oriented standards focused on enterprise value. Hence IFRS's work to further develop the prototype climate-related financial disclosure standards mentioned. Every board would do well to ensure that the company it oversees is familiar with this work.

Scenario modelling should be at the heart of all ESG disclosure. Judgments of materiality are often based on views of the past. But in today's fast-evolving society, what was material in the past may not be material now, and will be even less so in the future. Competent boards will ensure that management is looking ahead, and one of the best ways of doing that is with the help of scenarios. In the end, however, decisions on what is material to a company and its business strategy cannot be outsourced. Each board and management team must make its own judgment calls and be willing to sign off on them.

Measuring ESG Impact

Disclosure is an essential part of enabling outsiders to make an informed assessment of a company's ESG activities, but it is not sufficient. Investors, regulators, and others must also be able to measure those activities in a meaningful way, and to compare one company's record with its peers. Similarly, from the board's point of view, it is hard to exercise proper oversight if it cannot properly measure and compare the activities it is overseeing.

That said, measuring the impact of ESG policies has become a source of considerable frustration. The key accounting concept of materiality of financial information is, in itself, hard to nail down, even though it is now widely accepted that climate-related impacts on a company can be material and therefore require disclosure. To complicate matters further, companies must now also take account of "double and dynamic materiality." The EU views double materiality as a fundamental principle, under which companies need to consider not only the impact of climate change on themselves but also their impacts on the climate and, for that matter, other elements of sustainability. Dynamic materiality refers to the fact that an ESG issue may not be seen as financially material today but may become so in the future. These two materiality concepts are therefore related, and boards and investors alike would do well to ensure that they are monitored by their companies' risk management system. The issue of materiality is discussed in more detail in chapter 10.

Another problem is the low barriers to entry for creating rating and ranking systems, with the result that the market is now flooded with players offering such services—the World Benchmarking Alliance, Sustainalytics, MSCI, CDP, ISS, Bloomberg ESG Data, and Dow Jones Sustainability Index, to name some of the better known. The crowded marketplace creates not only confusion but also extra cost. Complaints are rife from companies that the time spent on responding to requests for ESG information more than outweighs the value they derive from the end product.

For the time being, boards would be well advised not to get caught up in the rivalries between different rating and ranking systems. Work with those that you and your key stakeholders trust. More important is that companies and their boards should be clear about their reason for participating in these services, namely, to figure out what they need to do better by asking questions such as: What does better mean? How can we do better? Is there a better process? Is there a better technology? Is there any wisdom out there that we need to acquire? As Mahindra's Ghosh notes: "Just putting out disclosures to say, 'Hey, we did better at this or we are better than so and so or we got a gold or a platinum' can be fun, but that's not the real purpose." Erika Karp, chief impact officer at Pathstone, an investment advisory firm, suggests another way for a board to measure ESG impact: ask what access the company is offering—whether it's access to education, access to water, access to broadband, access to mobility, access to clean energy, even access to animal welfare, and so on.

Accountability

Too often in the past, a company's strong words on ESG issues have not been matched by its actions, with the result that calls have grown for a greater measure of accountability. In this respect, the forceful letter written by BlackRock CEO Larry Fink in early 2020 should be a wake-up call for boards to ensure that they have the insight and information needed for proactive oversight of sustainability risks, opportunities, and disclosures. Fink's letter included this paragraph:

Where we feel companies and boards are not producing effective sustainability disclosures or implementing frameworks for managing these issues, we will hold board members accountable. Given the groundwork we have already laid engaging on disclosure, and the growing investment risks surrounding sustainability, we will be increasingly disposed to vote against management and board directors when companies are not making sufficient progress on sustainability-related disclosures and the business practices and plans underlying them.

As a first step towards bringing investors like BlackRock onside, boards should seek answers from management to four simple questions:

1. In coming years, will our customers and employees care more or less than they do today about the environmental and social impact of the company's products and actions? *(The board should expect that they will care more and question what management believes the key stakeholders will expect from the company's future products and actions.)*

2. Is the company currently making the most money from products that are solving environmental and social problems or from products that are contributing to those problems? *(The ratio will inform the board if or how fast a transition is needed.)*

3. What are the risks and opportunities for attracting and retaining talent with our current business strategy? *(The answer will determine if the strategy needs to be revisited.)*

4. What are the potential ESG and climate transition risks and opportunities for the company in the short, medium, and long run? *(The response should form a good basis for a strategic discussion.)*

Many boards, especially of larger companies, have found that an outside advisory body can be a valuable resource in helping them come to grips with their ESG obligations. The best advisory groups typically comprise experts in various fields, not necessarily directly related to the company's business. For example, Volkswagen's "sustainability council" established in 2016 includes the co-director of the Potsdam Institute for Climate Impact Research; the CEO of Systembolaget, a Swedish chain of liquor stores; a former president of the European Green faction in the European Parliament; a former EU commissioner for climate action; the founding director of UN Global Compact; a public policy expert at the Hong Kong University for Science and Technology; and the co-chair of the WHO/World Bank Global Preparedness Monitoring Board.

Advisory boards, however, are only useful when the directors and senior management are willing to make a serious commitment in time and engagement with its members. The best ones have a direct link to the company's formal governance structure so that the board of directors has a defined way to receive external input on matters beyond its own members' expertise. Even so, ultimate responsibility must lie with the directors themselves, as reflected in the fact that many boards are setting up ESG and sustainability committees.

CASE STUDY: INDITEX

The Spanish fashion retailer is a leader in an industry that is normally among the laggards in reputable ESG rankings. The company, which operates more than 6,800 stores around the world under brand names such as Zara, Pull&Bear, and Massimo Dutti, was ranked the number-one retailer in the Dow Jones Sustainability Index in 2018 and was still in the top ranks in 2021.[27] *Harvard Business Review* named its chief executive as the world's top performer, based on financial and ESG criteria.

Inditex has by no means escaped controversy. It was at the centre of a scandal over sweatshop conditions in 2011. A raid on one of its contractors in Brazil six years later found workers enduring unsanitary conditions for long periods of time. Labourers there were sewing notes in pockets stating, "I made this item you are going to buy, but I didn't get paid for it." But much has changed in recent years. Inditex announced in July 2019 that all its clothing would be made from sustainable fabrics by 2025, and that it would not use any fibres from endangered forests by 2023. Its stores no longer use plastic bags, and the company has pledged that 80 percent of the power used in its head office, stores, and factories will come from renewable sources. To ensure these goals are met, the company named a new head of sustainability, who works more closely with the CEO. As part of its response to the COVID-19 pandemic, Inditex said that it would close as many as 1,200 stores and shift its focus to online sales. However, it assured employees that the workforce would remain stable, and that those affected by the cutbacks would be offered other jobs, such as dispatching online purchases.

Inditex combines its financial results and ESG data in an integrated annual report, highlighting its environmental strategies, governance structure, and social responsibility. It has scored an AAA (leader) in MSCI's ESG rankings every year since 2016, with especially strong showings in privacy and data security, chemical safety, the carbon footprint of its products, and raw material sourcing. However, it remains to be seen whether younger generations will continue to support fast fashion or would prefer to swap used clothing with their peers, thereby undermining apparel retailers' current business model. Sweden's IKEA is already selling used furniture and encouraging customers not to send their old furniture to landfill. Many businesses will need to adjust in future to a circular economy model based on lifecycle analysis and more thoughtful research and design processes.

■ ■ ■

Guidelines for Competent Boards

» Ensure that every board member understands the importance of ESG issues and has a basic fluency in them. All directors should actively participate in board discussions on these topics.

» Establish an ESG governance structure and be sure to discuss ESG issues at all board meetings.

» Consider establishing a board committee overseeing ESG matters and, if beneficial, an ESG advisory board.

» Agree on the ESG factors that are most relevant to your business. Look not only to the past and the present but also to what may be material in the future.

» Examine shareholder and stakeholder expectations, then determine which ESG ratings, rankings, indices, and integration frameworks are most relevant for your company.

» Include ESG issues in risk-management systems and the company's risk matrix.

» Ensure that the board is kept up to date on external reporting initiatives. Understand what information is being provided, including that provided to rating and ranking organizations, and sign off on the reporting.

» Ask probing questions to ensure that management is considering all relevant outcomes, issues, and opportunities.

» Be sure to reap the innovation benefits that accompany ESG.

Ten Key Questions

(Recommended exercise: Ask each director to answer these questions independently. Then compare and discuss. More details on page 231.)

1. How does the company's business strategy align with material ESG issues and stakeholders' expectations?

2. Are you using ESG ratings, rankings, and indices to inform internal decisions? If not, should you be?

3. What risks and opportunities does the company's current business strategy create for attracting and retaining talent, customers, and capital?

4. How will new movements in society impact the company's ability to attract funds?

5. How is the board communicating with investors to determine what they want to see in the company's ESG disclosure and investor-relations materials?

6. What is the board doing to ensure that investors' expectations for material ESG disclosure match the company's actual disclosures?

7. Has the company taken proactive steps to ensure that its ESG disclosure (or lack thereof) will not invite legal action from plaintiffs, customers, investors, or others?

8. Which board members have the expertise to provide oversight on ESG? Who is held accountable for ESG performance? Is management held to account, and is that accountability tied to executive compensation?

9. Are board committee mandates suitably structured to include ESG issues?
10. Have the company's insurance policies—including directors and officers coverage—been reviewed in light of intensified scrutiny of ESG issues?

REFLECTIONS

"The world is so dynamic today that past experience does not always inform the future in the dominant way it used to, before the hyper-connected country and world we are today."

–Joyce Cacho, director, Sunrise Banks, NA

"It is within the responsibilities of trustees to analyze whether ESG issues are financially material, and to respond to these while understanding the views of their beneficiaries."

–Jessica Fries, executive chair, The Prince's Accounting for Sustainability Project (A4S)

CHAPTER 3

The Challenge of Climate Change

"If you really want to move towards zero carbon, you need to think in very concrete timelines. It has to go through more than just scenario planning; it has to become core to your annual work plan."

–Johan Rockström, director, Potsdam Institute for Climate Impact Research

WHY THIS MATTERS

No competent board can ignore the events that shook three of the world's mightiest oil companies during the week of May 24, 2021. At ExxonMobil, an activist investor succeeded in winning three board seats after a bruising proxy battle over the company's willingness to take a more aggressive approach to climate change. Chevron's shareholders rebelled against the board and management by backing a Dutch activist group's proposal to force the group to cut its carbon emissions. Across the Atlantic, a Dutch court ruled that Royal Dutch Shell's activities had contributed to climate change and ordered it to slash its carbon emissions 45 percent from 2019 levels by 2030. As if the upheavals at Exxon, Shell, and Chevron weren't enough, Australia's Federal Court ruled during the same week that the country's environment minister had a duty of care not to cause young people future physical harm from climate change.

These developments show how much has changed for the business world since Greta Thunberg, the Swedish teenage activist, delivered this harsh indictment in the fall of 2018: "To all of you who choose to look the other way … because you seem more frightened of the changes that can prevent catastrophic climate change than the catastrophic climate change itself: Your silence is worst of all." Fast-forward three years to June 2021, when climate change was a central issue at the meeting of the world's wealthiest nations in Cornwall, England. The leaders of the G7 industrial nations pledged to cut emissions in half by 2030 and to slow the rapid extinction of plants and animals caused by rising temperatures. They agreed to halt funding by 2022 for coal projects that lack carbon-capture technology and promised that the power generation sector would be "overwhelmingly decarbonized" by the end of the decade. That this would be judged as progress may sound strange in the not-so-distant future, but in 2021 it was indeed a step forward.

The combination of Thunberg's activism; an avalanche of scientific studies; a spate of deadly floods, droughts, and fires; and—not least—mounting pressure from investors and advocacy groups has now moved climate issues front and centre on boardroom agendas around the world. More and more companies are publicly pledging to reach a net-zero carbon emission target by the middle of the century or sooner. The drive to renewable sources of energy—chiefly, wind, solar, and hydro—is accelerating. The auto industry and its suppliers are rapidly shifting production from gasoline-powered cars and trucks in favour of electric vehicles.

All in all, the realization is rapidly taking hold that extreme weather events have become a major risk for business and a mounting cause for concern among investors and other stakeholders of what lies ahead. Heat waves, earthquakes, floods, droughts, and disastrous sea levels are already occurring with disturbing frequency. According to the United Nations Intergovernmental Panel on Climate Change's August 2021 report, these events will only get worse—much worse—altering the global economy, disrupting business operations and supply chains, and driving people from their homes.[28] A competent board would be foolish not to be weighing the many potential impacts of climate change: how it will affect procurement, production, and distribution, and how it will influence the actions of investors, business partners, and customers. As Jules Kortenhorst, chief executive of RMI, formerly Rocky Mountain Institute, puts it: "The energy transition is definitely accelerating. And for many in the sector, it will feel like a revolution. The pace of change that we're seeing at the moment in the energy sector is faster than anything we've ever seen before."

For corporate boards, the focus is shifting from how a company's activities impact climate to how climate will potentially impact the company's own financial performance. The impetus comes from multiple sources but, perhaps most important, from the financial sector. Andrew Steer, president and CEO of the Bezos Earth Fund, estimates that a quarter of financial institutions now take environmental, social, and governance issues into account in their decision-making. The blue-ribbon Task Force on Climate-related Financial Disclosures (TCFD), set up by the Financial Stability Board in 2015 and spearheaded by former Bank of England governor Mark Carney and former New York mayor Michael Bloomberg, has become an influential voice for promoting more informed investment, credit, and underwriting decisions, enabling a wide range of stakeholders to better understand the financial system's exposure to climate-related risks. In addition, companies can no longer ignore the growing involvement of regulators, especially in Europe, whether in the form of putting a price on carbon, setting progressively tighter standards for greenhouse gas emissions, or imposing tariffs on imported goods based on their carbon footprint.

Curtis Ravenel, a senior adviser to Mark Carney, the COP26 climate conference, and the TCFD Secretariat, sums up the pressures this way:

> Different actors—private, non-state, cities, states, companies, and various other players—are now in this "race to zero" where all these bodies are trying to commit to net-zero by 2050. They've created a number of vehicles under which the commitment can be validated, like new reports. The goal, at least in part, is to create headroom, show ambition from the private sector, fortify the policy-makers' ambition, and so forth. And you hopefully have continual development.
>
> If you're a board member, I expect you're going to get a lot of pressure from a number of different entities to make net-zero commitments. My advice is to make credible ones that include transition plans and are based on science. The

"race to zero" campaign will be a mad rush between now and COP to get as many people on this train as possible. And it will go on through 2050 as a permanent initiative within that COP process. What you'll see is a hardening of those net-zero expectations over the next several years. In some cases, we'll see jurisdictions not only make pledges to cut emissions like the US has but also actually legislate to cut emissions as we've seen with the EU.

Some sectors are adjusting faster than others. Solar and wind power are rapidly being integrated into electricity grids around the world. Battery technology is advancing so quickly that electric vehicles will soon be cheaper to produce than many gas-powered cars and trucks, not to mention having the advantage of lower maintenance, fuel, and insurance costs. While we can celebrate those improvements, companies and societies need to learn how to deal with the production of the new energy sources, as well as the cars and other products that will be scrapped as we transition to a net-zero economy. Boards need to ask management how business plans fit into a circular or regenerative economy, where the goal is to recycle and reuse without causing environmental and social harm. Some sectors, such as steel, cement, shipping, and aviation, are on the verge of discovering the technical solutions that will wean them off fossil fuels. The fact that they are working hard on reaching net-zero carbon emissions suggests that big changes lie ahead.

"For a lot of companies, the changes in the coming years are going to be so large that some will have to rethink their whole business model," says Peter Damgaard Jensen, who chairs the 330-member Institutional Investors Group on Climate Change.

"A board needs to have the capacity and capability to discuss this, and a strategy on how they would react to these changes."

Financial Times chief economics commentator Martin Wolf, among many others, sees the climate revolution as a "stupendous opportunity." Wolf explains:

> We have demands for social change and inclusion. These will create vast new opportunities. We also have a younger generation, younger than my children, who have different attitudes and values. The businesses that understand those new values and meet those new demands are going to have immense opportunities, while businesses that fail to do so will perish. Periods of difficulty and turmoil in the economy and society have often generated extraordinary social changes and business opportunities. This will be no exception.

HOW TO PREPARE

Corporate boards are accountable for the company's long-term resilience, and as the previous section makes clear, this includes adapting to the vast shift in the business landscape resulting from climate change. For boards, the climate crisis presents both threats and opportunities. Climate change will transform many, if not all, businesses—some for better, some for worse—and boards urgently need to consider how their companies will be affected. The impact is likely to be felt on many different fronts, among them:

- Lenders considering how to adjust the pricing on mortgages for properties at risk of flooding due to rising sea levels or more frequent extreme weather events.

- Insurance providers re-evaluating their coverage of property exposed to severe weather events and rising sea levels.

- The possibility of a vast expansion of grain production in areas such as the northern parts of the Canadian prairie provinces of Manitoba and Saskatchewan, while other areas lose their climate advantages for producing certain crops or wines.

- Technologies that enable cement and steel producers, among other industries, to operate without generating greenhouse gas emissions.

- Moves by governments to put a price on carbon emissions (see next section). Even the global shipping industry, which accounts for about 2 percent of greenhouse gas emissions but was not directly included in the Paris climate-change accord, issued a call in April 2021 for governments to tax its carbon emissions.[29]

"We are not talking about a silver bullet, but about silver buckshot," says Kortenhorst. "We have to do everything."

A Price on Carbon

A price on carbon—typically in the form of a carbon tax—uses the "polluter pays" principle to transfer the cost of the damage caused by climate change to the users of carbon-emitting products. Whether businesses like it or not, the reality is that governments around the world are moving in that direction by means of carbon-related taxes, carbon-trading schemes, and tighter restrictions on greenhouse gas emissions. The rising price on carbon will impose tangible—perhaps even crippling—costs on companies that fail to reduce their emissions, find innovative alternatives, or devise their own internal price mechanisms. On the other hand, boards eager to prepare for a low-carbon economy can make a positive impact by encouraging innovation, improving competitiveness, and ensuring long-term resilience. CDP estimated in 2020 that the number of companies using or planning to use an internal carbon price had soared by 80 percent in just five years, with more than 2,000 disclosing current or planned internal carbon pricing. Almost half (226) of the world's 500 biggest companies by market value were factoring the cost of carbon into their business plans.[30] According to Bezos Earth Fund's Andrew Steer, "The old economics of trade-offs has been debunked. We can now show that smart policies on climate change don't just stop bad things happening. They encourage greater resource efficiency, they drive new technology, and they lower risk. Combined, these lead to healthier economies, healthier profits, and healthier and happier citizens and workers."

As a first step, boards should make themselves aware of efforts to devise standard protocols that enable companies to account for and disclose carbon emissions. These range from requirements set by the TCFD to standards helping companies measure the carbon footprint of everything they buy and sell. One example is so-called Scope 1, Scope 2, and Scope 3 emissions, where Scope 1 refers to the direct emissions from owned or controlled sources; Scope 2 refers to indirect emissions from generation of purchased electricity, steam, heating, and cooling consumed; and Scope 3 refers to all other indirect emissions in a company's value chain. As Kortenhorst puts it:

> What is the carbon footprint of my mobile phone? What is the carbon footprint associated with turning on the light in my office? All these things suddenly become measurable. As a board, you want to know that your chief financial officer is appropriately accounting for money. Going forward, you will want to make sure that they are appropriately accounting for carbon emissions as well, which are just as important as the money.

However, rather than seeing carbon pricing as a threat, competent boards will tackle it as a challenge to do better. If done properly, a carbon pricing strategy should spur innovation and technological change, which in turn will lead to higher productivity, a sharper competitive edge, and long-term growth.

Follow the Science

Companies around the world are committing to the goal of net-zero carbon emissions. Few of them, however, have set targets based on science. In many cases, boards are asked to give the nod to a certain goal with little idea of how it will be achieved, how progress will be reported, or who will be responsible for implementing it. Some companies have set targets based mainly on what their competitors are doing, or what employees, customers, and investors are expecting. Some boards are justifiably afraid of being called out for greenwashing but approve the targets anyway, because "everyone else" is setting goals.

Combatting climate change is not about who can make the biggest promises, but about who can deliver net-zero solutions and report on them in a transparent and accountable manner.

The Science Based Targets initiative, a partnership between CDP, the UN Global Compact, World Resources Institute, and the World Wide Fund for Nature, says it is working with over 1,000 businesses to reduce their emissions in line with climate science. The initiative offers to make available a team of technical experts to review submissions from individual companies, validate them against science-based criteria, and communicate the evaluation with in-depth feedback. However, many, many more companies will have to sign on to such efforts to reach a net-zero carbon economy in a reasonable period. We need to stop greenwashing and green-wishing, and instead start green-walking—and competent boards need to ask questions and sign off on the targets as well as the plan and the budget needed to achieve them.

The Threats

The World Economic Forum's 2021 Global Risks Report lists "climate action failure" as the most impactful and second-most-likely long-term risk facing the world. "Climate change—to which no one is immune—continues to be a catastrophic risk," the report concludes. "Although lockdowns worldwide caused global emissions to fall in the first half of 2020, evidence from the 2008–2009 financial crisis warns that emissions could bounce back. A shift towards greener economies cannot be delayed until the shocks of the pandemic subside."[31]

Climate change raises several categories of risk that boards must assess, and then find ways of mitigating:

- Potential harm to assets and products. Investors are demanding that companies review the financial risks that they face from climate change and deal with the possibility that the value of some assets may decline dramatically in coming years. As long ago as 2013, a group of seventy money managers from around the world asked several dozen of the biggest oil and gas producers, coal miners, and power utilities to evaluate "the risks to unproduced reserves, due to factors such as carbon pricing, pollution and efficiency standards, removal of subsidies and/or reduced demand."[32] The demands have grown much louder since then, with more investors and advocacy groups seeking information on potentially stranded assets—and more boards complying with their requests. Every board needs to ask: Will climate change hurt us, and if so, in what way?

- Policy shifts designed to address climate change that, in the process, detrimentally affect a company's operations. These include carbon taxes, import restrictions, new curbs on greenhouse gas emissions, and more environmentally friendly product standards, such as restrictions or bans on single-use plastics.

- Access to finance. Banks and investors around the world are starting to factor climate change into decisions on providing and pricing capital. Take the shipping industry, where some ports are taking measures to curb emissions from vessels calling there. Clearly, a vessel that cannot meet the new requirements is worth less than one that can, a consideration that is sure to influence investors financing new ships. Likewise, the terms of loans for home construction and improvement are likely to be influenced by a project's sustainability. The Dutch bank ABN AMRO is training its mortgage advisers to help clients make their homes more environmentally friendly. Accenture estimated in May 2021 that 67 percent of US banks were prepared to direct capital away from the energy sector to assist in the transition to a low-carbon economy.[33]

- Access to talent. Companies with a poor record of adapting to climate change will find it more difficult to attract the best and brightest minds, especially among younger job seekers. A discussion of sustainability should be part of the hiring process, and sustainability should be embedded in training programs.

- Access to the raw materials and natural resources—notably water—essential to a company's operations. Even the most responsible company cannot remain in business if these ingredients are no longer available, or in short supply, or priced out of the market. A chocolate maker, for example, must have ready access to cocoa. Fish filled with bits of plastic or other toxins are useless to consumers and, by extension, to those that cater to them.

Boards that choose to turn a blind eye to these looming risks do so at their peril. Risks related to climate change were already among the top issues for investors during the 2020 and 2021 proxy seasons. Thus, the global investment firm Federated Hermes joined two of North America's biggest pension funds in sending an open letter to Berkshire Hathaway, the conglomerate controlled by veteran investor Warren Buffett, urging it to disclose how it is managing climate-related risks and opportunities, including climate-related financial reporting. The Berkshire Hathaway case also illustrates how investors are seeking more than a simple acknowledgment of climate risk, instead urging boards to integrate these risks into their business strategies, culture, and values. The Task Force on Climate-related Financial Disclosures (TCFD) as well as work now underway at the International Financial Reporting Standards (IFRS) Foundation calls for companies to assess the potential impact of different scenarios, including one that assumes a two-degree rise in global temperatures.[34]

The potential risks for boards are encapsulated in the 2015 Oslo Principles on Global Obligations to Reduce Climate Change, compiled by a group of experts from national and international courts, universities, and other organizations around the world.[35] The Oslo principles spell out the obligations of states and other parties to prevent further climate degradation. Boards that fail to live up to these responsibilities or to confront the risks mentioned above are in real danger of finding themselves on the wrong side of a wave of lawsuits, similar to those that engulfed asbestos manufacturers in the 1980s. David Pitt-Watson, co-founder and former chair of Hermes Focus Asset Management, describes the threat this way:

> We could be in a very sticky position in fifteen years' time if we have failed to address the climate problem. Naturally people will be looking for someone to blame. And they may go back to the Principles on Climate Obligations of Enterprises, or some other authoritative source and say: "You did not do this as a board of directors of the company. If not, I am going to sue your company." My sense is that if you've done nothing, they'd have a very good case in a world where we have not managed to get control of the climate. Thus even on a purely self-interested basis, climate has to be something that every board of directors thinks about.

Besides the threat of legal action, board members must take account of potential damage to their company's reputation and, indeed, themselves. A growing number of investors are already taking a stand by either voting against directors at companies perceived to be responding inadequately to climate change or, in some cases, divesting altogether. In August 2020, Storebrand, Norway's largest private fund manager, became the first sizable investor to dispose of holdings in businesses that continue to lobby against tougher environmental rules.[36] The fund's chief executive, Jan Erik Saugestad, noted: "Investors need to be responsible and proactive in accelerating the green transition. We are not passive actors awaiting the pending systemic harm that climate change will unleash." Storebrand has sold its stakes in more than twenty companies—mostly power utilities, chemical companies, and oil producers—that fall short of its climate policies. Among those policies is a commitment not to invest in companies that derive more than 5 percent of their revenues from coal or oil sands.

Across the Atlantic, US investors filed a record thirteen shareholder proposals targeting climate lobbying in 2021, up from four in 2020. Several noteworthy proxy victories followed in the 2021 proxy season. A proposal asking the chemicals producer DuPont to report on the amount of plastic it releases into the environment won 81.2 percent of votes, despite management opposition. Likewise, proposals seeking emission reduction targets at Phillips 66 and ConocoPhillips won 80.2 percent and 59.3 percent support, respectively.[37]

Job one in defusing these legal and reputational threats is adequate disclosure, says Carol Hansell, a Toronto-based adviser on governance issues. "The board and management need to capture the risks that climate change poses for their business, and articulate how those risks are being managed," Hansell says. Once that has been done, boards should investigate opportunities for dialogue and even collaboration with lenders, investors, customers, and possibly competitors to chart a path towards a lower or even zero-carbon future. Players in the steel and shipping industries, among others, are already moving in that direction. As a way of moving this process along, former Bank of England governor Mark Carney has suggested that the world's biggest banks should link executive pay to climate risk management.

The Opportunities

For many years, the climate-change debate, like the issue of sustainability generally, was framed around sacrifice. The assumption was that saving the planet from human abuse would have to come at the expense of economic development and, thus, corporate profits and shareholder value. Increasingly, however, the view is taking hold that, as Johan Rockström, director of the Potsdam Institute for Climate Impact Research, describes it, "the transformation towards a zero-carbon sustainable future is a journey that can generate more resilient, healthier, prosperous, and equitable economies, business, and society. Sustainability is increasingly seen as the entry point to successfully innovate."

For companies, this presents an opening to expand their customer base, find new sources of raw materials, and sharpen their competitive edge. "Over the last five years, remarkable new evidence has emerged suggesting that if you invest towards tomorrow's economy, rather than yesterday's economy, you'll actually do better, and you'll generate more jobs," says Andrew Steer. "If you spend the money on traditional things like roads and bridges and heavy chemical plants and private transportation, you will create a lot fewer jobs than if you invest in tomorrow's economy, in energy efficiency, renewable energy, and nature-based solutions."

The Global Commission on the Economy and Climate estimated in 2018 that a low-carbon economy could offer US$26 trillion worth of business opportunities.[38] Similarly, the International Energy Agency forecast in a 2021 report that clean-energy investments could attract US$4 trillion a year.[39] Mark Carney added ahead of the COP26 conference in Glasgow that the transition to net-zero emissions "is creating the greatest commercial opportunity of our age."[40] As Miranda Ballentine, chief executive of the Renewable Energy Buyers Alliance, points out, it is not only good for investors but also puts companies in a stronger negotiating position to adapt to new climate regulations.

The COVID-19 pandemic may hasten such innovation as policy-makers and business leaders realize that society is capable of far more dramatic adjustments than were considered feasible even in the recent past. The rapid rollout of vaccines and the explosion of remote working are two of the most obvious examples. The lesson for corporate boards is that change does not have to happen gradually but can be swift and disruptive. "The fact that we now realize it is possible for us to raise our game more dramatically than we thought, that's really good news," says Steer.

Energy costs are a great place to start. Managements typically do not consider energy as an expense that can be controlled, instead assuming that costs will inexorably rise by a certain amount over a period of time. But technology is advancing so quickly that there is an ever-growing opportunity for improving energy efficiency, thereby cutting energy costs and reducing the firm's carbon footprint. What's more, clean-energy costs today are often at or below those of fossil-fuel power, providing another strong incentive for change.

The search for ways to combat climate change does not have to be a grinding, bureaucratic exercise. With a bit of imagination, it can be both enjoyable and rewarding. Instead of just planting trees, a company could examine new carbon-capture equipment that does the work of a thousand trees. "Hopefully you like to have a little fun as a group, and start thinking outside the box with your leadership team on how can you set your company up to be successful twenty and thirty years from now," says Ballentine. "The fun part about being a board member is thinking about what we can create. How can we create a market before the next guy down the line does it?"

CASE STUDY: NRG ENERGY INC.

The climate debate has whipsawed Houston, Texas–based NRG Energy in recent years, offering some sobering lessons to every board considering the implications of climate change.

NRG was the US's second-largest electricity producer in 2017, with about 23 gigawatts of generating capacity in California, Texas, and eastern states, based largely on coal-fired power. The company is classified as an independent power producer, selling electricity directly to utilities and users. But the profits of many independent producers have sagged over the past decade due to the wide availability of cheaper renewable energy sources combined with flattening demand for electricity.

NRG initially sought to counter this trend by moving into the clean-energy industry under the leadership of David Crane, a well-known proponent of renewable energy. Crane favoured a sweeping transformation of the company that would move it away from fossil-fuel power generation towards solar and other renewable energy sources. "The day is coming," he wrote in a letter to shareholders in 2014, "when our children sit us down in our dotage, look us straight in the eye, with an acute sense of betrayal and disappointment in theirs, and whisper to us, 'You knew … and you didn't do anything about it. Why?'"[41]

However, Crane was abruptly fired in 2015, and in contrast to many of its peers, NRG's drive to a clean-energy future stalled. But the market did not stand still. In Texas, one of NRG's strongholds, wind has overtaken coal to become the second-largest energy source. NRG published a report showing all but two of the state's fifteen coal-fired generators were losing money.[42] The company's current CEO, Mauricio Gutierrez, has acknowledged that "the independent power producer model is now obsolete and unable to create value over the long term."[43]

With investors and customers demanding a greater exposure to renewables, NRG was left with few options but to change course once again. Activist investors forced a restructuring in 2017. In response, the company announced a three-year transformation plan that included up to US$4 billion in asset sales, US$13 billion in debt reduction, and US$1 billion in cost savings.[44]

While NRG's non-renewable–focused strategy may have created short-term value for shareholders in the past, the board now realizes that it must foster growth in renewable energy capacity to capitalize on opportunities that favour more sustainable options. In 2019, the company began to embrace wind and solar as part of its portfolio.[45] As a result of these moves, NRG's share price began to climb again after years of under-performance. As of 2021, the company was accelerating its sustainability program and greenhouse gas reductions. It reported a 55 percent drop in greenhouse gas emissions since 2014 and said it had contracted more than 1.8 gigawatts of renewable energy supplies for customers, "with more on the horizon."[46]

■ ■ ■

Guidelines for Competent Boards

» Acknowledge that climate change will have a far-reaching impact on your company's operations and culture.

» Familiarize yourself with the Task Force on Climate-related Financial Disclosure (TCFD) and its recommendations. Use the task force's work as a guide for internal discussions on scenarios, strategies, risks, and targets.

» Get ready to report your company's progress in tackling climate change as TCFD reporting becomes mandatory or embedded into accounting standards.

» Ensure that management has identified the company's short- and long-term climate risks and opportunities and has drawn up strategies to manage them.

» Accept carbon pricing as a reality, then see it as an opportunity for innovation rather than as a threat.

» Ensure that the company's lobbying activities and advertising are aligned with its climate policies.

» Work with lenders, suppliers, employees, and customers to find ways of mitigating climate-change risks.

» Identify activities that can transition the company towards net-zero operations.

» Use the TCFD, the SEC's 10-K form in the United States, and similar regulatory reports in other countries to disclose as much information as possible on the company's climate policies and scenarios.

» Release a statement, signed by the CEO and board members, confirming that all have read and discussed the IPCC 2021 report.[47] The statement should explain whether and how the report has prompted a change in strategic plans and priorities.

Ten Key Questions

(Recommended exercise: Ask each director to answer these questions independently. Then compare and discuss. More details on page 231.)

1. Do members of your board consider the risks and opportunities of climate change as an integral part of their accountability for the long-term steward-ship of the company? How so? Which of you have the expertise to provide oversight on climate mitigation and adaptation strategies?

2. How does the company assess the financial, supply chain, and reputational risks of climate change?

3. How often does the board consider different scenarios to assess the potential consequences of climate

change on the business, and the business's impact on society?

4. Has the company signed onto science-based net-zero carbon commitments, and drawn up plans and budgets to achieve those goals?

5. Does the company have any assets that could be considered stranded in the foreseeable future? Are you committed to winding down those assets rather than selling them to a buyer that might do even more harm to the environment?

6. How do you and your board remain informed about sound climate-governance practices?

7. How does your board ensure that climate risks and opportunities are being adequately discussed with investors?

8. Is the board kept informed about the company's spending on energy? Does management consider energy a controllable operating expense?

9. Are science-based climate targets integrated into management incentives?

10. Is the board's position on climate change aligned with the company's lobbying and marketing messages, and its membership in trade associations?

REFLECTIONS

"This is not just doom and gloom, but we have a way to make different choices from the ones that got us into this trouble. These choices are not, as people typically think, only sacrifices. We know there are business opportunities. There are new industries that can be built. There are opportunities for existing industries and companies to change their portfolio."

–Peter Schlosser, vice-president, Julie Ann Wrigley Global Futures Laboratory, Arizona State University

CHAPTER 4

SDGs: Ignore Them at Your Peril

"If you look into the national SDG plans, it's like looking through a big catalogue of investment and export opportunities. So this is another example that doing good and doing well is an integrated process these days."

–Torben Möger Pedersen, CEO, PensionDanmark

WHY THIS MATTERS

Almost every government in the world, 193 in all, came together in 2015 to adopt a blueprint for global peace and prosperity known as the 2030 Agenda for Sustainable Development. At the core of the initiative were 17 ambitious "sustainable development goals," or SDGs, that amount to a call for action to end poverty and other deprivations by improving health and education, reducing inequalities, and spurring economic growth, while also tackling climate change and preserving the earth's oceans and forests. Given that the 17 goals reflect the aspirations of billions of people, they have come to colour discussions and implementation of a host of policies, both at the national and international level. That process involves not only governments but also businesses, investors, community leaders, and, indeed, anyone in a position to influence the direction of our lives.

The SDGs have galvanized environmental, fair trade, anti-poverty, and renewable energy activists, among many others. From the point of view of business, more and more owners of capital are deciding that they wish to leave a legacy that amounts to more than how much money they made on this earth. This shift has helped spawn the growth of sustainable finance, which is no longer an outlier in capital markets but increasingly part of the mainstream. What's more, as interest in this concept of impact investing grows, so too do the financial, environmental, and social returns of SDG-friendly ventures previously viewed as offering little financial reward.

The 17 SDGs represent the world's biggest threats, but also hold the promise of rich returns.

On one hand, no business can succeed in a world that fails. No board member or CEO can make money or keep their job if their business burns to the ground, is swamped by an entirely foreseeable flood, or has lost the confidence of those who put their trust in it. The SDGs have all but settled the debate on which direction the world needs to take in years to come, and the only thing yet to be determined is the speed and scale of commitment, plus the accountability that comes with it. Boards that fail to integrate the SDGs into their overall strategies could thus find themselves exposed to severe regulatory and reputational risks. However, companies and boards that embrace the UN targets stand to be well rewarded. Competent boards would be wise to act, and act soon, to move their companies towards solving the world's biggest pain points. In the process, they will help cement their own licence to operate and grow.

THE 2030 SUSTAINABLE DEVELOPMENT GOALS[48]

1. End poverty in all its forms everywhere.
2. End hunger, achieve food security and improved nutrition, and promote sustainable agriculture.
3. Ensure healthy lives and promote well-being for all at all ages.
4. Ensure inclusive and equitable quality education, and promote lifelong learning opportunities for all.
5. Achieve gender equality and empower all women and girls.
6. Ensure availability and sustainable management of water and sanitation for all.
7. Ensure access to affordable, reliable, sustainable, and modern energy for all.
8. Promote sustained, inclusive, and sustainable economic growth, full and productive employment, and decent work for all.
9. Build resilient infrastructure, promote inclusive and sustainable industrialization, and foster innovation.
10. Reduce inequality within and among countries.
11. Make cities and human settlements inclusive, safe, resilient, and sustainable.
12. Ensure sustainable consumption and production patterns.
13. Take urgent action to combat climate change and its impacts.
14. Conserve and sustainably use the oceans, seas, and marine resources for sustainable development.
15. Protect, restore, and promote sustainable use of terrestrial ecosystems, sustainably manage forests, combat desertification, and halt and reverse land degradation and halt biodiversity loss.
16. Promote peaceful and inclusive societies for sustainable development, provide access to justice for all, and build effective, accountable and inclusive institutions at all levels.

17. Strengthen the means of implementation and revitalize the global partnership for sustainable development.

HOW TO PREPARE

The revenues of the world's corporations are much higher than those of governments, non-profits, or charities, giving business an unmatched capacity to invest and generate revenues in a way that benefits local communities, individuals, and the planet as a whole. In other words, action by business will play a major role in determining whether we can achieve the goals, and how soon. Plus, no company is too small to make a contribution. This chapter outlines the benefits and the risks of pursuing the SDGs and proposes some ways to help boards move forward.

Opportunities for Innovation

Many countries have designed national programs to help them achieve the UN development goals. These create innumerable openings for businesses of all kinds. The Business & Sustainable Development Commission estimates that implementing the 17 SDGs could be worth at least US$12 trillion a year in market opportunities and create 380 million new jobs.[49] Companies that understand the scale of the opportunity and take steps to act on it will reap enormous benefits. Paul Polman, Unilever's former CEO, observes:

> I would like a new CEO that I appointed to any business to at least be aware of these opportunities. The Business

& Sustainable Development Commission report went to about 1,800 CEOs, and many are acting on it now by integrating it into their sustainability strategy, or even into their overall corporate strategy.

Guided by the board, a company, large or small, can construct a useful long-term business forecast by identifying the SDGs most relevant to its strategy, as well as the various national programs linked to each goal. This exercise can help pinpoint likely winners and losers as governments move towards implementing the SDGs. Much the same principles apply to investors as they decide how to allocate capital. Keith Martell, CEO of First Nations Bank of Canada, notes that "if you're seen as a good place to put money because you're not into short termism, if you can show that you've got superior returns because you're not covering the costs of the bad practices that don't accomplish the SDGs, then you're a good place to invest."

A Competitive Advantage

The language of sustainable development has become a global one, spoken by governments, investors, business, employees, lenders, and suppliers, in other words, by almost every one of a company's stakeholders. The 17 SDGs can thus be a powerful tool for boards and managers to communicate their strategies and goals in a consistent and effective way. On the other hand, if your company shies away from acknowledging the UN targets, it risks being left behind in some of the most promising areas of economic development—renewable energy, electric vehicles, tourism, and agriculture, to name a few.

CDP's Paul Dickinson puts it this way:

> There is no greater democracy than the way citizens around the world invest their money and spend their money. And they are increasingly showing that they're not interested in creating problems for themselves or their children by buying the wrong thing from the wrong people. So you put sustainable development on the board agenda, and you never take it off. And that's going to be great for you. It's going to give you a material competitive advantage in a fast-evolving field.

Not long ago, businesses would measure their social responsibility performance using yardsticks such as the number of tables they bought at a charity golf tournament or their contribution to the local opera company, without thinking how it relates to the company's strategy or purpose. But the growing attention to sustainable development in general and the 17 UN goals in particular has opened the door to a far broader and more strategic approach, engaging many more stakeholders and, probably, winning far more recognition. And the benefits do not end there, given growing evidence that a commitment to sustainable development draws in new customers, attracts smart employees, and secures the loyalty of suppliers.

The first step in making such a commitment is to pick a few of the 17 goals where the business can make the biggest impact. Boards should ask where they have an opportunity for positive impact, and where they need to shrink or eliminate the business's negative impact. The company can then explain what it plans to do, when it plans to do it, and which financial and other resources it has allocated, bearing in mind that such initiatives are likely to be measured not in months, but in years and perhaps even decades. Therefore, this process is an opportunity to set specific short- and long-term targets, explain risks, and, if necessary, temper expectations. The process helps investors and analysts, as well as other stake-holders, track progress, while also proactively defusing future criticism, thus becoming a powerful communications tool for both the board and management.

Reputations at Risk

Besides the risk of missing out on vast opportunities, companies that fail to embrace the SDGs could find themselves struggling to defend their brands and their reputations. Young people in particular are demanding to know what an organization's stance is on broader social and environmental issues. Many of these youngsters—and a growing number of investors, too—are less excited by a company that slashes costs by 30 percent or moves production from a high-cost to a low-cost country than by one that is helping to combat climate change or improve community health in some impoverished part of the world. These shifting priorities are also reflected in moves by governments to bring policies into line with the 17 SDGs through measures such as bans on single-use plastics, higher minimum wages, and gender-diversity rules, among many others. Firms that fail to keep abreast of these changes are sure to find themselves lagging behind their more nimble rivals.

In the future, the onus will be on businesses to show that they are not just producing stuff and making money but also doing some good for society as a way of making money. This applies especially in parts of the world that were once viewed by many Western companies simply as emerging markets, ripe for the picking. "Gone are the days when you would just come to the continent and do what you want," says Emily Waita Macharia, Coca-Cola's director of public relations in Africa. She continues:

> The region has matured, and it is much keener to ensure that it protects its resources. There's a lot of focus on accountability and governance. Governments are hounding any organizations that do not comply with local legislation, and the way we are moving, we're going to continue seeing a more aggressive regulatory environment.

Regrettably, however, much of the progress made in meeting the UN's goals has eroded during the COVID-19 pandemic. For the first time in two decades, the number of people living in extreme poverty has risen. Hundreds of millions of jobs have been lost or reduced. Women, in particular, have taken a hard hit, reversing decades of narrowing inequality in the workplace. Ironically, one of the few signs of progress has been a reduction in greenhouse gas emissions.[50]

This fast-changing landscape means that boards need to look at the SDGs as part of their company's core business, rather than as a separate initiative, a side activity, or a philanthropic endeavour. As Ingvild Sørensen, senior program manager at the UN Global Compact, sees it:

> As with any communication and any sustainability strategy, there's a huge difference between those who use the SDGs for greenwashing, easy wins, cherry-picking, or whatever you want to call it, compared to those who

actually take it in as part of the core business. And that really shines through.

When sustainability is embedded into the core business, you see the benefits of having a better track record with your employees and your suppliers on societal and environmental issues. All these things have just become more important. If you're doing well on those, it's going to benefit your business, whereas if you just use them for nice pictures in your annual report, you probably won't see the same return.

CASE STUDY: NOVOZYMES

Novozymes, based outside Copenhagen, Denmark, is the world's largest supplier of industrial enzymes and microbes. Its products help reduce water and energy consumption, and its customers include many of the world's leading consumer product manufacturers, such as Unilever and Procter & Gamble. It was also the first company in the world to publish an integrated financial, environmental, and social annual report.

Since becoming an independent company in 2000, Novozymes has harnessed sustainability to its business strategy in three distinct phases:

- Initially, its priority was to cement a reputation as a socially responsible company, for example, by keeping operations and supply chains on a sustainable track and by reducing energy and water consumption, and other costs.

- In 2009, after talks with big customers such as Walmart, "we believed it was really time to step up in terms of what sustainability could do for our company," recalls Claus Stig Pedersen, head of global sustainability. "We tried to find how we could meaningfully integrate sustainability into all corners of our business—in sales, marketing, investor relations, stakeholder engagements, communications, and many other business functions."

- Starting in 2014, Novozymes became one of the first companies in the world to use the UN's sustainable development goals, in Pedersen's words, "to inform our corporate strategy and target setting." It set about forging partnerships and collaborative ventures to maximize that impact.

One immediate payoff was the positive attention that Novozymes attracted from business schools and the media as a role model for other companies. "Our employees also loved that there was positive attention around the company," Pedersen adds.

At the same time, however, the company could not lose sight of the need to remain profitable. To that end, it built an assessment tool that integrated aspects of the SDGs with life-cycle assessments of its products, so that it could better understand the correlation between the goals, Novozymes's technologies, and opportunities for innovation. It identified several areas where it could contribute to the SDGs, such as the use of bioenergy in transportation. The next step was to discuss with policy-makers around the world, notably in Brazil,

China, and India, what regulatory changes would be needed to introduce these new technologies.

The company went a step further in 2018, setting up an open innovation platform and inviting entrepreneurs to come up with fresh ideas on how biological technologies could help meet the sustainable development goals. Novozymes chooses the best submissions, and then gives its chosen partners access to its enzymes and microbes to help develop commercially viable products.

The company has also set up two groups, known as the SDG impact board and the SDG foundation board, that set targets, priorities, and strategies to meet the UN goals. One group aims to develop products that will help customers make the biggest possible impact on meeting the SDGs. The other works closely with suppliers to minimize the negative impact of their products and processes on sustainability. A new initiative, known as "better business with biology" was launched in mid-2020 with the purpose of harnessing sustainable business practices to meet the planet's future needs.

Novozymes's commitment to the SDGs, Pedersen says, has paid off in numerous ways: contented employees, communities that trust the company, customers willing to talk about innovation, and open doors to regulators. "We can clearly see there is a big need for many changes in the world in the coming decade to meet the global goals," he adds. "We are doing our part to help create the waves of change. But these things are going way too slowly. We need to move much faster."

■■■

Guidelines for Competent Boards

» Identify the specific UN sustainable development goals (SDGs) most relevant to your company's business and embed them in your strategy, based on where they could have the greatest impact.

» Put the SDGs on the board agenda and never take them off. Keep asking what risks and opportunities they present.

» Decide which performance indicators to use to measure progress and ensure accountability.

» Evaluate and benchmark all investment and product development decisions against the SDGs.

» While the SDGs set targets for 2030, think ahead to potential risks in 2050. Among the possibilities: biodiversity loss, scarcity of natural resources, and disruptions stemming from climate change, cybersecurity, and data privacy risks.

» Explain to outsiders how your company is contributing to the sustainable development goals. Be sincere and realistic about where you are—in terms of both the problem and the solution.

» Encourage partnerships with suitable outside parties.

» Encourage—even better, inspire—board members, management, and stakeholders to set and achieve SDG targets on their own or in partnerships.

Ten Key Questions

(Recommended exercise: Ask each director to answer these questions independently. Then compare and discuss. More details on page 231.)

1. Which board members are familiar with the UN's sustainable development goals?
2. How often does the board discuss risks and opportunities related to the UN's sustainable development goals?
3. Is your company seen as part of the solution to sustainable development or part of the problem? Does perception match reality?
4. Which of the 17 SDGs are most relevant to your business, and to current and future stakeholders? Where do you have the most positive and negative impact?
5. How could those SDGs integrated into your company's long-term strategy and culture be used to attract a broader range of investors, employees, and other key stakeholders?
6. How are the SDGs included in your company's scenario planning and in R&D and investment planning?
7. How often do you consider the cost of a lost/missed opportunity due to not embracing the SDGs?
8. Is management doing enough to spur innovation and create new business opportunities based on the SDGs?
9. Have you set up internal reporting processes and performance indicators to track implementation of the SDGs?

10. Are processes in place to ensure appropriate accountability in implementing SDG-related initiatives—including in your company's risk management processes?

REFLECTIONS

"As you start to break down those 17 SDGs, you realize that each one of them relates in some way, shape, or form to issues that businesses can have an impact in changing, either for better or worse, through their actions. By far, corporations have the biggest capacity and capability to both invest and generate revenue in a way that has a material impact on people, planet, and society."

–Upkar Arora, board member, chair of the Risk Committee, Vancity Community Investment Bank

CHAPTER 5

Pain in the Supply Chain

"Companies are now discovering that you might
  outsource your value chain, but you cannot outsource
  your responsibilities."

–Paul Polman, former CEO, Unilever

WHY THIS MATTERS

Among the crises that can blindside even the most competent
boards, few match the far-reaching consequences of allegations that a company or its suppliers are guilty of abusing
human rights. Just ask Nike, which had to pull US$100 mil-
lion worth of soccer balls from stores on the eve of the 1996
World Cup after news broke that one of its suppliers was
employing Pakistani children to stitch the balls.

Until quite recently, companies typically responded to
such accusations with a promise to investigate and a dis-
claimer that suppliers' behaviour was not their responsibility.
From a legal point of view, that stance may have seemed
adequate and correct. However, that is no longer the case.
Customers, employees, politicians, investors, regulators, and
the public at large are now demanding a more aggressive and
proactive approach. Numerous countries have adopted rules
aimed at combatting child labour, forced labour, and similar

human-rights abuses. Codes of conduct and monitoring devices of various kinds have proliferated. More generally, companies in North America and Europe are increasingly expected to answer for the practices of their suppliers—and even their suppliers' suppliers—no matter where they happen to be. In 2017, France became the first country to pass a "duty of care" law holding multinationals criminally responsible for human-rights or environmental violations at their subsidiaries and suppliers. Since then, several other countries, like Germany and the Netherlands, have followed suit, and there is little doubt that more will do so over the next few years.

Gerry Tidd, executive vice-president of BlueScope, Australia's largest steelmaker, and chair of ResponsibleSteel, notes:

> Increasingly, our customers—for example, developers or urban planners or architects—specify what they want so they can claim a six-star rating for their buildings. They want to know that the steel is quality steel in the sense that it's sustainable steel. That's where our customers are increasingly taking us. And that's where we'll go.

Some businesses have responded more enthusiastically than others, often depending on the degree of scrutiny they face from outsiders. Among the most active have been apparel retailers, whose success in the marketplace depends on maintaining the goodwill of their customers. Likewise, agri-food producers buy huge quantities of commodities such as coffee, cocoa, and palm oil from developing countries and have come under mounting pressure from activists and governments to address environmental and human-rights abuses in their supply chains. The French cosmetics maker L'Oréal now chooses almost 90 percent of its suppliers based on environmental and social performance.[51] What these companies have in common is a realization that while they may not have a legal obligation to tackle society's wider problems, failure to do so adds a huge risk to their business in the form of damage to their brands and reputation.

The COVID-19 pandemic has brought a long list of supply-chain challenges. Disruptions in supplies and sharp swings in demand forced companies to lay off tens of millions of workers around the world, leaving many of them without any income, and without basic needs such as food and shelter. Meanwhile, some businesses fortunate enough to see a spike in demand for their products were forcing workers to return to factories without proper protective equipment or other safety measures. The pandemic has also put a new spotlight on workers' mental health, with stress not only affecting their productivity but also likely causing a sharp rise in domestic violence. On another front, it has raised fresh concerns about the substandard living and working conditions of migrant workers. Their plight has caught the eye not only of progressive businesses, but also of activists who can quickly turn these issues into the kind of public controversy that every board and CEO would prefer to avoid.

More generally, the pandemic has encouraged companies to take a new look at their supply arrangements. With borders closed and numerous restrictions in place, questions have arisen about the efficiency of far-flung global supply chains. Competent boards should, at the very least, be considering whether to consolidate the number and geographical spread of their suppliers, and the consequences of doing so. As Michael Kobori, Starbucks's chief sustainability officer, sees it:

> Pre-COVID, global supply chains were very consolidated and dependent on precise forecasts of demand. They were generally not vertically integrated, which meant no one supplier controlled every stage from raw materials through to the finished product. There were many, many hand-offs and a large network of suppliers. As we have seen through COVID, if any link in that chain is broken, the entire supply chain is disrupted. It's not a very resilient system. In many ways, it's quite a fragile system. I believe that in order to improve resiliency, there will be a decentralization of supply chains. There will be redundancies built in. There will be literally more slack built into the system.
>
> It's actually the supply chains of smaller- and medium-sized enterprises that are surviving, because they've been forced to operate on the margin, outside of those big global, consolidated supply chains. So out of necessity, they've been forced to be more nimble and more agile.

HOW TO PREPARE

Addressing human-rights abuses, pollution, and other supplier malpractices may be an essential part of a board's mandate, but taking action can be far from easy. For many businesses, supply chains are more like supply webs, operating at multiple levels with many intricate relationships. Often the thorniest problems arise not with the largest suppliers at the top of the pile but with those further down—and perhaps further away—on whom the company is equally dependent but with whom it has less contact and thus less influence. Exploitative suppliers can also be wily adversaries. It takes every tool available, often involving considerable time and cost, to gather evidence of exploitation, and then act on it. On the other side of the coin, the proliferation of smartphones and social media provides the means for workplace abuses to be quickly exposed and disseminated. An unprepared board can quickly find itself caught in the vortex of a crisis.

A competent board needs to consider that suppliers' exploitative practices are all too often the result of ever-tougher demands from their customers, especially for lower prices. Directors can't have it both ways: on one hand, demanding from management that all suppliers adhere to an ESG code of conduct, while on the other, expecting the procurement department to buy the lowest-cost products with the shortest delivery times. They would be well advised to follow the example of companies such as IKEA which have discovered that they can use their purchasing power as a force for good, reducing both costs and risks.

A good starting point is for boards to insist that management treat suppliers as partners with a shared purpose and strategy. A relationship of this kind helps foster trust and loyalty, with both sides taking a similar approach to issues such as the environment and labour practices and adhering to mutually agreed-upon standards. At the heart of this approach is the realization that the buyer is often responsible for a supplier's behaviour. Eager to win and keep business, savvy suppliers will be glad to fit in with their customers' priorities, including explicit standards for labour conditions and industrial pollution or, more broadly, a commitment to the UN's sustainable development goals and commitments to reducing their carbon footprint.

The board's job is to oversee this shift from a focus on short-term monetary cost to the importance of environmental, social, and governance issues. It must ensure that the company has the proper processes and review mechanisms in place to effectively monitor implementation. That includes vetting new and existing suppliers to determine their ethical standards and their commitment to sustainable development and diversity. New technologies are making that task much easier. For example, blockchain can be used as a digital transaction ledger to record the movement of goods, thereby improving transparency and accountability. Some companies are now publicly identifying their suppliers, and monitoring organizations have compiled databases to track suppliers' ethical and sustainability performance.[52] In the end, however, appropriate training for suppliers can pay bigger dividends than punitive monitoring systems and penalties.

John Manley, the Business Council of Canada's former CEO who has also served on several corporate boards, sums up the board's obligation this way:

> You've got to go to management and say, "Satisfy us that we have steps in place that we know where things are coming from, and that if there's a factory fire in, say, Bangladesh, that it's not going to reflect on us or our direct workers." You need to ask if our suppliers are safe and if they are maintaining proper standards, because if not, it will come back to hit the company. It's part of the responsibility of a board to ensure that those questions can be answered to their satisfaction.

Revamping Supply Chains

Supply chains are sensitive not only to the traditional forces of trade and business but also increasingly to ESG issues such as climate change and human-rights abuses. This shift suggests that every board needs to take a close look at potential vulnerabilities to its company's supply chain, and to mandate and oversee whatever changes may be necessary. Thus, many companies are concluding that supply chains should be shorter and less complex than they have been in the recent past. Equally important, customers need to hold suppliers to the same standards as they hold themselves.

Besides bringing improvements in reputation and productivity, a revamped supply chain can also spur innovation. Michael Kobori, Starbucks's chief sustainability officer, recalls the time when his former employer Levi Strauss was looking for ways to reduce the hazardous chemicals used by suppliers to bring out the worn, bleached look for which Levi jeans are famous. It discovered not only that lasers could do the same job as the chemicals but also that the time to finish the product could be shortened from hours to just a few minutes. What's more, the laser process enabled the company to delay decisions on final products until much later in the process, thus radically reducing its lead times from more than six months to as fast as weeks or days in some cases. The process brought the added benefits of lower inventories and being able to customize jeans closer to the market where they were being sold. "So that sustainability constraint led to innovation that had multiple business benefits," Kobori notes.

Walking away from an errant supplier is not necessarily the answer since it can create more problems than it solves. The supplier will have little incentive to improve its labour and environmental practices, and its workers may be left worse off than before. Instead of summarily severing a relationship when a supplier falls short, a company can seek to negotiate an action plan for improvement in areas of poor performance. Andrew Wallis, who heads Unseen and Modern Slavery Help-line, an anti-slavery group, urges companies to team up with their peers to apply pressure on suppliers: "If you go with your competitors and say, 'These are our minimum standards that need to be applied,' then you've got leverage because they still want your business." Wallis and many others point out that the ideal is to forge long-term partnerships with suppliers built on trust, stability, and a clear understanding of the customer's expectations.

Monitoring Supplier Performance

As pressure has grown for more responsible and sustainable supply chains, so have demands for greater transparency in suppliers' performance. As a result, monitoring mechanisms of various kinds are becoming the order of the day. Whether boards like it or not, public opinion is firmly on the side of stepping up monitoring of supplier performance. Among consumers, younger generations, notably millennials and GenZs, are looking for brands and products that reflect their values. They want to know the provenance of the goods and services they spend their money on. Much the same applies to job seekers, who are increasingly aware of the ESG credentials of prospective employers. Competent boards should be familiar with monitoring options relevant to their firm's circumstances and should work to implement them if they wish to avoid unflattering publicity and possibly even legal action.

Gathering data from suppliers is key, and this process highlights the importance of a mutually respectful partnership between supplier and customer. The goal is to strengthen the supplier by working together to reduce costs in a sustainable way. In the event of a crisis and the threat of unfavourable publicity, a company should be in a situation where it can trust its suppliers to be upholding acceptable social and environmental standards. Boards should thus ensure that monitoring mechanisms are rigorous and reliable. Nancy Lockhart, a director of George Weston, a Canadian food group, has this advice:

> You've got to make sure that you've got boots on the ground paid by you, who are auditing and regulating what goes on in the field. You can't be everywhere, you can't go behind every factory door, and you can't be sure that people aren't going to be dishonest. But you've got to put as many measures in place as you can to ensure that you can do an audit that will uncover any issues that put the company at risk or put people at risk.

Governments and other stakeholders have adopted or are considering an array of measures to bring supply chains under closer scrutiny. Among those in effect by mid-2021:

- France passed a duty of vigilance law in 2017 requiring companies to report on environmental and human violations in their global supply chains. Under the duty-of-care principle, victims of breaches can seek damages.[53] Since the law came into force, four lawsuits and four notices had been filed, as of mid-2021.[54] Several other countries, including Germany and the Netherlands, have subsequently passed similar legislation.[55]

- In 2019, the Netherlands adopted a law that requires companies to determine if child labour has been used to make their products and, if so, how to eliminate it. Companies must submit statements to the government on their due diligence.[56]

- The European Parliament adopted a resolution in March 2021 containing recommendations to the European Commission on corporate due diligence and accountability.

- The UK's Modern Slavery Act, passed in 2015, consolidated slavery and human trafficking offences and introduced new preventive measures, support systems, and a regulatory body. The law provides for both trafficking reparation orders under which seized assets can be used to compensate victims and prevention orders to ensure that those who pose a risk of committing modern slavery offences cannot work in relevant fields. Companies with annual sales of more than £36 million with operations in the United Kingdom must publish an annual compliance statement.

- California's Transparency in Supply Chains Act, signed in 2010, requires large retailers and manufacturers to spell out their efforts to eradicate slavery and human trafficking from direct supply chains for any goods they offer for sale in the state.[57]

- The United Kingdom, the United States, and Canada unveiled new measures in early 2021 in response to alleged human-rights violations in Xinjiang, China. The UK called for strengthened operation of its Modern Slavery Act; the US issued a "withhold release order" against certain products from the Xinjiang region; and Canada adopted similar measures to bar goods originating there.[58]

- A group of financial institutions subscribe to the Equator Principles, which set out a framework for assessing and managing environmental and social risks in projects. The principles are intended to provide a minimum standard for due diligence and monitoring to support responsible risk decision-making. As of mid-2021, 118 financial institutions in 37 countries had adopted the principles.[59]

- Beyond strictly legal obligations, a number of "soft law" initiatives, notably the human rights provisions of the United Nations Global Compact and the UN Guiding Principles on Business and Human Rights, have created a framework for corporate policies that respect and support internationally recognized human rights.

What does this mean in practice? Kristina Touzenis, managing partner at BST Impact, has this advice for dealing with suppliers:

It actually doesn't matter if you have the fanciest, most robust policy in place but you don't have the accompanying internal governance mechanism. Let's say that you produce T-shirts or you sell T-shirts produced in a country that is known for not respecting workers' rights. The first thing you can say is: we are aware of this right now; we are engaging our supply chain and finding out how they're actually creating these T-shirts. Then you put in place a system for engagement with your suppliers, and what you want to see from them. It could be a living wage, or maximum hours of work, or health and safety measures. You can even do something really small, such as having a doctor come and visit your labour force and their families once a month in an area where access to health care is scarce or difficult.

And then you can say in your reporting, "We have identified these issues with the suppliers. We are engaging them instead of just cutting them off, because if we give them six or twelve months to put systems in place, that actually protects the workers." You can add: "However, we have no idea where our cotton comes from. We are planning to engage the cotton producers once we have identified them." So it's also about not being afraid of not being perfect from one day to another, because that's just not possible.

HOW TO FORGE A SOUND RELATIONSHIP WITH SUPPLIERS: ONE EXPERT'S VIEW

If you create the right mindset on the part of management and leadership, then that begins to impact the operations and the practices of your suppliers. You enter longer-term relationships, and you have an incentive to maintain a positive relationship over many years. I remember at Levi Strauss & Co., many of the supplier relationships stretched back ten or fifteen years. With that kind of long-standing relationship, it's not a single-period game where you're simply trying to maximize that particular transaction and see how much you can get from the other party. It's a multi-period game where you are both invested in building the kind of partnership that leads to business success on both sides. It sounds somewhat idealistic, but it is a shift that has occurred in the apparel supply chain among the larger brands and retailers over the past few years.

"One reason is that companies are asking their suppliers to do more. It's no longer a case of just delivering a quality product on time at a reasonable cost. Now, there are environmental requirements, there are labour requirements, there are all kinds of management systems that brands are asking for. A small, individual factory cannot hope to meet those kinds of requirements any more. So we have moved to an era of large or mega-vendors that themselves are multi-million-dollar companies with their own network of factories in multiple countries. That is how supply chains are beginning to evolve."

—*Michael Kobori, chief sustainability officer, Starbucks*

CASE STUDY: TOP GLOVE

If evidence was needed that even companies with stellar reputations can find themselves plunged into an ESG crisis, consider the case of Top Glove, the world's largest maker of rubber gloves. Headquartered in Kuala Lumpur, Malaysia, Top Glove ticks many of the right ESG boxes, and its record on environmental, social, and governance issues is prominently displayed on its website.

The company has pledged that its water treatment plant will emit no carbon by 2022 and that its offices will follow suit by 2025. More than two-thirds of its natural rubber latex suppliers are certified by the Forest Stewardship Council. Five of its twelve directors are women, and its independent directors are limited to a nine-year term. Working overtime is voluntary for its 22,000 employees. And so on. *HR Asia* magazine named it the continent's best employer in 2021 for the fifth year running.

Demand for Top Glove's products soared during the COVID-19 pandemic as health-care workers around the world took extra precautions to protect themselves from infection. Its share price surged sixfold during the first twelve months of the pandemic, making its founder and chair, Lim Wee Chai, Malaysia's eighth wealthiest person, according to *Forbes* magazine. However, the share price as well as the company's earnings later fell back as vaccines were rolled out and the company faced stiffer competition from low-cost rivals in China.

To make matters worse, the day after the latest *HR Asia* award was announced in March 2021, US Customs and Border Protection ordered the seizure of Top Glove products arriving at US ports. Shortly afterwards, the agency seized a shipment of almost four million gloves.

The crackdown followed years of allegations that Malaysian glove makers have used forced labour in their operations. The US agency said that it had found evidence of debt bondage, excessive overtime, abusive working and living conditions, and retention of workers' identity documents by the company. A Top Glove worker died of COVID-19 in 2020 after an outbreak of the virus in the company's factories and worker dormitories, which Malaysian authorities alleged were uncomfortable, cramped, and lacking proper ventilation. In July 2021, the US Department of State downgraded Malaysia to the lowest ranking in its annual report on human trafficking.

Top Glove has sought to dispel the concerns over its labour practices. At the time the United States announced its ban, the company, which was housing nearly 12,000 foreign workers in Malaysia, said that it was investing 200 million Malaysian ringgit in new dormitories. It insisted that conditions in the hostels complied with or exceeded the requirements set by a new law on workers' housing that took effect in 2020.[60]

Lim said in June 2021 that the company had addressed the US government's concerns and was "just

waiting" for Customs and Border Protection to verify
its remediation practices. The company cited a report by an ethical trade consultancy that it had hired
to verify its labour practices. The US agency told the
Financial Times it was in talks with Top Glove and said
that import bans of the kind imposed on the company
were only lifted when there was proof forced labour
was no longer used.

■ ■ ■

Guidelines for Competent Boards

» Consider whether you can reconfigure your supply chain to build resilience and to enable training as well as closer monitoring of contractors and subcontractors.

» Forge long-term partnerships with suppliers based on mutual trust and respect.

» Bear in mind the reputational risks of a relentless push for lower prices and demanding deadlines.

» Keep questioning management's policies and processes to ensure respect for human rights and responsible sourcing of supplies. Check that management is complying with relevant legal requirements, and is aware of proposed laws and regulations in the pipeline.

» Familiarize yourself with relevant industry codes of conduct and government regulations relating to human-rights, labour, and environmental issues.

» Work with trusted community groups and non-governmental organizations (NGOs) to understand local conditions and potential trouble spots.

» Align the power of procurement with incentives for suppliers.

Ten Key Questions

(Recommended exercise: Ask each director to answer these questions independently. Then compare and discuss. More details on page 231.)

1. Which board members have the expertise to exercise oversight on supply-chain and human-rights issues? Which of them is responsible for these matters?

2. How does the company choose and work with suppliers?

3. What governance structure has the company put in place to manage human-rights and other supply-chain issues?

4. What relationships does the company have with NGOs and other experts on the ground?

5. Has the company communicated expectations for suppliers through a responsible sourcing code of conduct? Has training been offered?

6. Does the company have a system in place to ensure that potential violations among suppliers are suitably addressed?

7. Does the board know what is *really* going on in the supply chain? For example, is the company doing spot audits and unannounced inspections?

8. Are incentives in place to encourage supplier compliance with company policies?

9. Are you confident that management is complying with relevant legal requirements, and is aware of regulatory developments that may apply to the company?

10. Should the supply-chain strategy be revamped as a result of lessons learned during the COVID-19 pandemic?

REFLECTIONS

"I want you, as a member of the board, to be able to look your kids in the eye and say, 'Through my work and through my business, we actually made the world a better place.'"

–*Andrew Wallis, CEO, Unseen and Modern Slavery Helpline*

CHAPTER 6

Male, Pale ... and Stale

"A paper exercise that works extremely well is to say, 'This afternoon, every one of you is going to come up with a succession plan where you can only present a female person to replace you,' And then repeat the same exercise with candidates only from minority backgrounds. If you find that there is a skills gap in your candidate, you have your action plan right there. That will force the manager to look at his or her team and realize where the gaps are in their pipeline."

–Francesca Ecsery, non-executive director

WHY THIS MATTERS

If proof is needed of how diversity can boost a business, consider what happened seventy years ago when Earl Tupper launched his plastic Wonder Bowl, the very first Tupperware product. A pioneer of modern lifestyle design, the new bowl was widely praised for its light weight and affordable cost. Yet department stores battled to sell it because housewives— as homemakers were then known—preferred to cling to their old glass jars and ceramic containers, distrustful of the Wonder Bowl's unfamiliar seal. Their doubts quickly melted, however, after Brownie Wise, a former Miami secretary and advice columnist, began recruiting women to sell Tupperware products at "Poly-T parties" in their homes. By the early 1950s, Wonder Bowl sales were booming, and Tupper had recruited Wise as his company's first female sales chief.

Tapping into the talents that women offer is now just one dimension of an accelerating drive to promote diversity, equity, and inclusion in the workplace, including the boardroom. For several decades after Brownie Wise joined Tupperware, boards had little appreciation of the full scope or value of these concepts, apart from the benefits of more women in the workforce. However, awareness has grown that diversity takes many forms, including gender and gender identity, race and ethnicity, sexual orientation, socio-economic status, disability, age, religious and spiritual beliefs, and lived experiences. Corporate leaders began to give serious attention to diversity in the 1980s, but it is only in the last few years that we have begun talking about equity in the workplace, in other words, an acknowledgment that some people start with less advantage and privilege than others, making it much harder for them to succeed.

The benefits that flow from a culture of diversity, equity, and inclusion are significant, and well documented by research. Diversity creates a virtuous circle. For starters, it is a rich and valuable source of information, and it drives a more inclusive and equitable culture, leading to more productive discussions, better decisions, and, in the end, improved outcomes. It enhances the ability to attract and retain the best talent. Beyond the confines of the company, diversity sends a powerful message to customers and suppliers, boosting the brand and inspiring loyalty and trust. McKinsey & Company reported in 2020 that companies in the top quartile of gender and ethnic diversity on their executive teams were, respectively, 25 percent and 36 percent more likely to enjoy above-average profitability than those in the bottom quartile.[61]

But most boards have yet to appreciate the scope of diversity and the advantages it brings. Business leaders are still inclined, for instance, to overlook the wisdom, not to mention the marketing and branding opportunities, that emanate from the 1.3 billion people on the planet with disabilities. "There's still a mindset among business leaders that disability is an issue for governments, or a medical issue," says Caroline Casey, founder of The Valuable 500, a group of companies and leaders committed to disability inclusion. "It isn't understood in a way that business can see the value, insight, innovation, and opportunity this global market represents."

Catalyst, a non-profit, has found that companies with the highest representation of women on their top management teams experience stronger financial performance, including a 35 percent higher return on equity, than those with the lowest representation of women.[62] Similarly, Coqual, formerly the Center for Talent Innovation, has estimated that organizations highly rated for diversity, equity, and inclusion are more likely to succeed in new markets and to improve their market share.[63] A study by the online decision-making platform Cloverpop has found that diverse teams (based on age, gender, and geography) are up to 87 percent more likely to make the right decisions.[64] What's more, when teams follow an inclusive process, they typically make decisions twice as fast at half the number of meetings.

No board can afford to close its eyes to these benefits, and pressure is mounting on those that do. A 2021 EY survey has found that almost half of all investors believe diversity of board, management, and workforce should be a strategic priority.[65] The reason for this growing awareness is simple: board members are responsible for ensuring that the corporation meets its potential. That applies not only to the present but also to the future, underlining the need for investment in education and other measures of well-being in local communities. Without a clear commitment to diversity, equity and inclusion, boards are failing to take full advantage of the human assets—whether workers, consumers, or suppliers—that a company has at its disposal. The pervasive influence of online platforms such as Twitter and Glassdoor means there is no place to hide from disgruntled employees. In other words, if your company continues to turn its back on diversity, equity, and inclusion, don't be surprised if employee discontent erupts on social media, and perhaps even leads to legal action.

HOW TO PREPARE

Diversity, equity and inclusion start in the boardroom, and the essential first step is to ensure that the makeup of the board itself reflects diverse and complementary perspectives. As noted above, diverse boards lead to more productive discussions and challenge silo thinking. They also enable boards to better understand the needs of stakeholders, support innovation, and manage complex issues.

Paul Druckman, chair of the World Benchmarking Alliance, notes that the point of diversity is not only about a variety of physical attributes but also, and more importantly, about a rich mixture of ideas and experiences. "It can't just be people who have done similar sorts of things in other companies, even if they're different genders from different companies," Druckman says. "It needs to be people from outside of the comfort zone." Thus, a board member specializing in artificial intelligence or blockchain or cyber risk would look at a business quite differently than would a financial or legal expert. Combining these backgrounds and skills can create a formidable competitive advantage. The same applies to first-time board members. Most companies look for directors with board experience, yet I hear more and more often from asset managers that they would prefer novices who ask seemingly "naïve" but vital questions that veterans may not have thought of.

Peter Dey, chair of Paradigm Capital and former chair of the Ontario Securities Commission, adds:

> You don't want people who all think the same way. In reaching a decision, you want people who end up together with a consensus. But that consensus should reflect a compromise of a range of views and a range of experience. If you can't bring the board together, then that's a problem. That's where leadership and compromise are important.

Wes Hall, executive chair of shareholder services firm Kingsdale Advisors, urges an even more fundamental change in the selection process. All too often, he notes, management plays the most influential role in choosing new directors, which means that "you're not going to select someone who's very tough, and who is going to be hard on you and hold you accountable. You're going to select people who you feel you can kind of get to do what you want, or who will maybe let things slide a bit." In Hall's view, "the whole process of selection of directors should change."

Sure enough, the composition of boards is starting to shift in the direction of diversity, thanks to a combination of far-sighted leadership and regulatory demands. One especially momentous advance came in December 2020 with a proposal by the National Association of Securities Dealers Automated Quotations exchange, commonly known as Nasdaq, that at least two members of the board of every one of the 3,100 companies listed on the exchange cannot be straight white men.[66] In most cases, one must be a woman and the other a member of an under-represented minority or LGBTQ. The SEC approved the proposal in August 2021.

"There are so many great, qualified candidates waiting to go on corporate boards," Nasdaq's CEO Adena Friedman told *Fortune's* "Leadership Next" podcast after the announcement: "It's an exciting time to give more and more people an opportunity to be part of the corporate environment." Friedman noted that 85 percent of the 200 comments on the proposal submitted to the Securities and Exchange Commission were positive, many of them from prominent investor groups and companies. Nasdaq has also offered to help listed companies find suitable board candidates. "The governance of companies matters in terms of risk controls and financial performance, and therefore diversity is an important component of that," Friedman added.

At its core, the push for diversity, equity, and inclusion is about changing the corporate culture. Julie Gebauer, global head of human capital and benefits at consultancy Willis Towers Watson, explains the challenge for boards:

Creating an inclusive culture takes time, a roadmap, committed leadership, and steady attention. And finally, accountability. The acceptance and embrace of difference must be woven into the fabric of the organization, reinforced by leaders, managers, and peers, and supported by programs and policies. An inclusive culture not only implements programs that support diversity, like flexible work arrangements, sponsorship programs, and inclusion networks, but also has managers who know how to use them. In an inclusive culture, managers find ways to ensure that people of all backgrounds can contribute. They ensure that differences are understood and embraced. While data metrics, targets, and culture are all essential ingredients, they must be accompanied by leadership accountability for making progress toward diversity goals, and for creating an environment where everyone can succeed.

According to Gebauer, the most effective leaders make their commitment to an inclusive and diverse culture evident in three ways. First, the language they use must be modern and conscious of pronoun choices. Second, their decisions must reflect that commitment—for example, not only filling leadership slots with a mix of candidates but also ensuring that initiatives and opportunities are offered beyond traditional groups. Third, leaders must uphold the standards they espouse by ensuring that only appropriate behaviours are rewarded. As Gebauer puts it, competent boards

> set total reward programs that meet the needs and expectations of a diverse talent population, like paid parental leave and fertility services and voluntary benefits that support

flexibility and choice. They ensure talent programs and policies—like recruiting and promotion processes—are free of unconscious bias, and they debunk the myths that have excused inaction in the past.

Shifting the corporate culture towards diversity, equity, and inclusion takes time—often a long time. The process needs to encompass both the obvious, such as bringing more women, minority groups, and people with disabilities onto the board and senior management, as well as more nuanced initiatives, such as making sure that job descriptions do not contain unconscious biases. That may require setting up new networking initiatives, identifying suitable role models and mentorship programs, and changing sponsorship policies, among many other adjustments.

Two Crucial Roles: Chair and Nominating Committee

If the start of a transformation in culture lies with the board, then the impetus for that transformation must come from the chair and the nominating committee. Their priority should be the appointment of new members to the board, a move that some of their fellow-directors may find hard to stomach. The chair can make that task far easier by regularly reaching out to investors for their views, and then using their input to persuade other members of the board of the need for change. The chair should also consider involving suppliers and representatives of key communities, not necessarily at the board table but perhaps as members of an advisory stakeholder council. Giving these outside parties a voice will likely help both smooth and speed up the transformation process.

The nominating committee plays a critical role in defining the board evaluation process and ensuring that unconscious biases are avoided. It must also ensure that a rigorous process for assessment of candidates for board positions is in place to discourage "checking the boxes" and to avoid tokenism. No company can justify avoiding or delaying new board appointments by using the excuse that it cannot find suitably talented candidates among women, visible minorities, people with disabilities, and other traditionally disadvantaged groups. To get the job done, the chair and the nominating committee must look beyond the usual pool of candidates, going out of their way to hunt down fresh talent. One way of doing this is to devise a board competency matrix that identifies skills gaps in the current board and reduces the risk of bias, conscious or otherwise, in the selection process. Two valuable resources for this exercise are the "Directors' Playbook" published by the Canadian Gender and Good Governance Alliance,[67] and the UK Equality and Human Rights Commission's "Good Equality Practice for Employers" guide.[68]

Changing the composition of the board is just the start of the transformation process. A competent chair must then encourage diversity of thought and ensure that no opinions or questions remain unspoken. More than that, the chair has a special responsibility to ensure that new members are not set up to fail, in much the same way as a chief executive would support a company's first black or female vice-president. To illustrate the point, Leslie Traub, principal consultant at Udarta Consulting, tells a powerful story involving one of her assignments at a North American bottling company:

I'm in this auditorium for the whole day with the top ninety people. There is one brown-skinned woman. She comes up to me at lunch and says, "I just want you to know I was enticed to come here from another company after twenty-five years where I was at the top of my game. I've been here for eight months, and no one has ever asked me to lunch. I thought this would be my last company. This is the loneliest I've ever been."

Traub describes some important takeaways for boards from this encounter:

I've worked with a number of boards that pat themselves on the back for their diversity. But when I get in there and I interview the board members who are young, of colour, and women, and we talk about the dynamics on the board, they say that they aren't being heard, that their contributions aren't valued, and that the decision-making happens after-hours. It's very difficult if you're the only one, because then, in a way, you're a token. If you're two, you're a cabal. But if you're three, you can be listened to and heard as individuals. It's incumbent on people in the dominant culture, wherever you are in the world, to recognize the dynamics of what it's like to be the only one, or one of two. And it's also incumbent on you, as the board chair, to make sure that you're getting the full contribution from all your talent.

Accountability and Performance Evaluation

As mentioned, introducing a culture of diversity, equity, and inclusion can be a long and arduous process. More than that, as with any attempt to change long-standing practices, the initiative is sure to garner an enthusiastic response in some quarters but skepticism and outright resistance in others. An implementation plan is obviously necessary, but momentum can be maintained only by measuring performance and insisting on accountability. Agreed targets and policies must be followed, and the board must have sufficient oversight to ensure accountability.

As part of the accountability process, the board should review progress towards diversity and inclusion at regular intervals, preferably each quarter. Numerous performance measurement mechanisms are available. Among the most popular is the Global Diversity, Equity and Inclusion Benchmarks, devised by the Centre for Global Inclusion based in Las Vegas. The benchmark comprises a scorecard with fourteen different categories, each measured on a scale of five, starting with inactive and moving up to reactive, proactive, progressive, and best-in-class. Some boards also lay down specific rules to encourage diversity, for example, insisting that both a male and a female candidate must always be considered for certain middle-management and senior positions. Another effective way of holding directors and senior managers accountable is to tie diversity goals to financial incentives. Managers must understand that their bonuses may be smaller or even disappear if they fail to meet specified targets.

The monitoring and accountability process should extend to outsiders with whom the company does business, such as auditors, advertising agencies, and suppliers. Ideally, these parties should compile reports on diversity, gender pay gaps, and so on within their own ranks. By publicizing these reports at least internally, a company can help raise awareness of these issues. The bottom line is that further investigation is called for if a company is not reaping the benefits that diversity makes possible.

Data Is Key

Boards should oversee diversity, equity, and inclusion initiatives in the same way as any other important program, using targets, data, and benchmarks to measure progress on key fronts. Gebauer's advice is to start with data on workforce demographics, especially categories considered important to the company. If the main concern is women at senior levels, the board should ask for data on gender distribution at each level and in each division to capture a picture of the most critical gaps and the pipeline of potential candidates to fill them. More and more companies are also using pay-equity reviews as a starting point for deeper analysis of diversity and inclusion initiatives, followed by planning and action.

The goal is to ensure that men and women, people of different ethnicities, and people with disabilities receive similar compensation for comparable roles. Setting specific targets should be a key part of this process. One tip: data for all groups should be segregated by gender, given that there can be a big difference between, for example, a South Asian man and a Black woman in terms of pay and advancement opportunities. The board should also insist on seeing any benchmarks that may be available as gauges of overall progress in the marketplace. Succession planning should be an area of special interest for the board.

Besides hard data, the best way for board members to get a feel for what's right and what's wrong with the corporate culture is to talk to employees. Traub advises:

> If it's a business you're willing to support, and the culture isn't there, then this is where you have to gather together your C-suite and ask, "What are we doing about the culture?" I would start by asking if those beautiful values posted on the front of your board book are actually lived. Values can often be aspirational. But to what extent are they really part of the fabric of the organization? Symbolism is important, but symbolism and window-dressing only get you so far.

An Overlooked Constituency

Critiques of diversity typically focus on gaps in gender and ethnicity. However, competent boards also need to pay attention to age diversity, in particular the adequate representation of young people at all levels in the organization, including the board itself. Businesses of all kinds are coming to realize that millennials born between roughly 1981 and 1995 have a very different outlook from baby boomers born between 1946 and 1964. Their approach to work is different, as reflected in their expectations of employers and of themselves. Giving full voice to these differences can lead to a transformation of a company's culture and business strategy, especially in sectors geared towards consumer products and services.

Despite these seemingly obvious benefits, the age composition of US boards has changed little. According to Spencer Stuart, an executive search firm, the average age of new S&P 500 independent directors was 57.8 in 2020, more than a year older than the average of 56.5 in 2010.[69] Furthermore, the average age of all S&P 500 independent directors, at 63, had remained unchanged since 2009. Only 17 percent of incoming S&P 500 directors were 50 or younger in 2020, but a third of them brought technology-sector experience, a critical attribute these days. A 2018 PwC survey found that more than one in five directors were older than 75.[70] Ten percent of them were over 80, which, astonishingly, was roughly double the proportion under 40. Every board should seriously consider welcoming some millennials to its ranks, even if it is just one individual who is not afraid to make his or her voice heard. Maureen Metcalf, founder and chief executive of the Innovative Leadership Institute, notes that "there are young folks who are developmentally incredibly advanced, and seem to be going through the levels more quickly."

Equally important is that members of the board, no matter what their age, retain a youthful perspective on their company and the world around them. As Cynthia Cherrey, chief executive of the International Leadership Association, puts it: "Having a mindset that is global is so critical. Being able to think holistically and to think in systems and how things are connected to each other are important today for board members and CEOs."

CASE STUDY: STATE STREET GLOBAL ADVISORS

On International Women's Day in 2017, the Boston-based asset manager State Street Global Advisors, in partnership with advertising agency McCann New York, erected a 50-inch bronze statue of a defiant girl in front of Wall Street's famous charging-bull statue. Dubbed the Fearless Girl, the installation was designed to drive home a powerful message to corporate America. Fearless Girl was part of State Street's campaign to pressure companies into adding more women to their boards. Following the installation, State Street wrote a letter to many companies that comprise the Russell 3000 index, urging them to expand the diversity of their boards.[71] Since 2017, the statue has travelled to many cities around the world, such as London, Melbourne, Oslo, and Cape Town, to spread the message on board diversity and challenge outdated corporate thinking.

By early 2021, 862 of the 1,486 companies State Street identified as lacking gender diversity at the board level had either added more female directors or committed to do so in the future. State Street's president and CEO Cyrus Taraporevala announced in his 2021 letter to directors that racial and ethnic diversity together with risks associated with climate change would be the fund manager's top stewardship priorities for 2021.[72] State Street intends, he wrote, "to hold boards and management accountable for progress on providing enhanced transparency and reporting on these two critical topics." He also revealed that State Street was tightening its proxy voting rules for 2021 and 2022. For example, in 2021, it pledged to vote against chairs of nominating and governance committees at S&P 500 and FTSE100 companies that fail to disclose the racial and ethnic composition of their boards. In 2022, it plans to vote against these chairs if the company does not have at least one director from an under-represented community on its board.

By July 2019, every S&P 500 company had one or more women on its board. General Motors, Bed Bath & Beyond, Casey's General Stores, Viacom, CBS, and Omnicom Group, among others, now have more female than male directors. Nonetheless, as of November 2020, only three S&P 500 companies had women occupying a majority of senior management roles. As of mid-2021, women were at the helm of only 6 percent of S&P 500 companies, only 11 percent of top earners were women, and women held just 21 percent of all board seats.[73] While the shift towards board diversity may be in motion, PwC's 2020 annual corporate directors' survey indicated that fewer than half of directors surveyed (47 percent) thought that gender equality was important for their boards, while only a third said the same about racial diversity.[74]

These results suggest that most boards need to become far more assertive in addressing diversity. If they fail to do so, they risk being propelled in that direction anyway by a broadening array of players, whether stock exchanges, asset managers, employees, customers, or initiatives such as the Fearless Girl campaign.

Guidelines for Competent Boards

» Bear in mind the difference between diversity, equity, and inclusion. Be sure that company policies cover all three.

» Collect data and analyze it. Measure it against relevant benchmarks, whether those are your competitors, industry peers, or others in your country or region.

» Acknowledge that transforming the corporate culture is key. A good place to start is the composition of the board and senior management team.

» Recognize the particularly important roles of the chair and the nominating committee. Make sure they are able to make informed decisions on diversity, equity, and inclusion.

» Be sure to have adequate representation of young people (i.e., those under 40) on the board and in senior management.

» Ensure that leaders, especially those representing minority groups, are encouraged to take on board positions to gain more insight and improve the pipeline of competent board candidates.

» Go beyond symbolic gestures such as grandiose vision statements. They will get you only so far. Action must follow.

» Keep a close watch on activist demands and regulatory changes, even if they do not apply directly to your company. What looks like fringe activity today could be mainstream requirements tomorrow.

Ten Key Questions

(Recommended exercise: Ask each director to answer these questions independently. Then compare and discuss. More details on page 231.)

1. Does your board understand the business case for diversity, equity, and inclusion?
2. Are directors included in diversity training programs, including those related to emotional intelligence and unconscious bias?
3. Have management and the board made statements of commitment to diversity, equity, and inclusion both in and outside the company? Are these intentions reflected in the company's products, advertisements, and behaviour?
4. Is time regularly set aside during board meetings to discuss and monitor progress on diversity, equity, and inclusion?
5. Has your company set short- and long-term diversity targets that impact recruitment, retention, development, and succession strategies across all functions and levels, including the board?
6. Does your company link compensation directly to diversity, inclusive practices, and equitable behaviour?
7. Does your company provide equal wages, hours, and benefits for all employees for equal work?
8. Does your company offer flexible work options, including start/end times, work location, leave and re-entry opportunities?

9. Does your company have a zero-tolerance policy towards all forms of discrimination and workplace violence, including sexual harassment? How do you oversee that policy?
10. Has your board considered term limits for directors? Are you open to appointing first-time board members?

REFLECTIONS

"From a capabilities perspective, what we should be looking for in the future is compassionate leadership. I use 'compassion' intentionally because there's a very important difference between empathetic leadership, or emotional intelligence, and compassionate leadership. Empathy doesn't move you to action. Compassionate leadership does."

–Nabeela Ixtabalan, chief people and corporate affairs officer, Walmart Canada

CHAPTER 7

Just Say No

"You should never be in a situation where you agree to do something wrong because it feels right. Because in the future, it will come back to bite you. To have paid a bribe or paid someone to benefit your company because it felt like you were doing the right thing at that moment ... it was unlawful and you shouldn't have done it."

–Claudia Sender, director of several prominent European and Brazilian companies

WHY THIS MATTERS

Make no mistake, corruption—whether practised by your own company or by others—can take a devastating toll on careers, on reputations, and, in the most extreme cases, on a company's very survival. Gone are the days when a public accountancy exam like my own might include a question on how much a company can deduct for bribes. Now, more and more countries are clamping down on corruption in all its forms. Some, such as the United Stated, the United Kingdom, and Canada, are extending enforcement beyond their own borders. Momentum is building for suppliers, joint-venture partners, and investors to demand proof of compliance with anti-corruption programs as a condition of doing business.

In most-recent moves, more than one hundred leaders from forty countries signed a joint declaration in June 2021 urging the creation of a new international anti-corruption court.[75] At about the same time, the United Nations Office on Drugs and Crime launched the GlobE Network (Global Operational Network of Anti-Corruption Law Enforcement Authorities) to strengthen international cooperation against corruption, while President Joe Biden has pledged to make the fight against corruption a core US security priority.

The message is getting through to the business world. "There's a lot more sensitivity today around issues of corporate ethics, misconduct, and sustainability," says José Hernandez, chief executive of Ortus Strategies, a Zurich-based crisis management consultancy. "The old attitude of 'everyone else is doing it, so it's okay for me to do it' is becoming less and less tenable. In its place, there's a growing understanding that if we're working for a large global brand, we must take a firm stand against misconduct to protect our reputation."

One important reason for this shift—and one that competent boards dare not lose sight of—is that public opinion around the world is taking a far harsher view of corruption. Demands to root out corruption are growing louder, and with them, the number of investigations and prosecutions is rising. Even in countries that have a long history of looking the other way when improper payments are made to government officials, ordinary citizens have become increasingly aware of how corruption exacerbates income inequality, violence, and other social ills.

For companies, this means that allegations of corruption pose an increasingly real business risk. While we normally associate bribes, money laundering, and similar malpractices with developing countries, the problem has surfaced with growing frequency in the industrial economies. Almost three-quarters of respondents to a March 2021 survey by KPMG's Australian arm reported that the risk of fraud and corruption had risen during the pandemic, and 85 percent said that they did not expect that risk to diminish during 2021.[76] When a company chooses not to be transparent about corruption, it risks being exposed by others. The costs can be devastating in terms of permits and licences revoked, mergers and acquisitions put on hold, properties seized, employees jailed, guilty companies blacklisted from doing business with specific institutions or countries, and, not least, the incalculable cost of diminished public trust. More than that, bribes have an insidious though often hidden cost on the people, the economy, and the communities where the company and its corrupt business partners operate.

The good news is that the "halo effects" of transparency and integrity are also becoming more apparent. Companies with a reputation for straight dealing typically enjoy easier access to capital markets and can expect greater loyalty from their employees. Governments that clamp down on corruption are likely to be more stable, with more generous social programs and less civil unrest. Hernandez notes that "in general, people do not want to be associated with brands that have neglected ethics in pursuit of other goals. On the contrary, having a reputation for compliance, ethics, and sustainability can give a strong boost to the public perception of your company's products, services, and overall stature in the marketplace."

HOW TO PREPARE

Organizations all too often allow themselves to slip into unethical behaviour without being fully aware of the consequences. The slippery slope starts with minor mistakes and misjudgments, which balloon into a bigger problem as the board and management rationalize whatever steps they take to try and correct the situation. Before long, the organization can find itself in the grip of a full-blown crisis where it has overstepped the bounds of not only ethical but also legal behaviour. Financial statements are manipulated; bribes are paid to win contracts; and money is laundered to hide ill-gotten gains. One reason for this snowballing effect is that white-collar criminals often start off as trusted insiders and star performers who are willing to cross the line either for competitive reasons or to boost their own egos. If an employee's performance seems too good to be true, that could be less a reason for celebration than a warning sign that merits further investigation.

The task of maintaining high ethical standards and preventing mistakes from turning into scandals rests on two main pillars: a strong culture of transparency and integrity, and appropriate policies and controls. As discussed below, the board can—and should—play a critical role in putting both these elements in place. Both need to be approached in a systematic way with vigilance and commitment. They involve everything from training to vetting suppliers and subcontractors, and to setting firm rules—all with an eye towards detecting, deterring, and limiting exposure to bribery and other ethical abuses. The drive to stamp out corruption also underscores the need for diversity on the board and in senior management. Some studies have concluded that having more women in elected office and on corporate boards leads to lower levels of corruption, though others suggest that opportunity and exposure are more potent triggers, whatever the gender of the perpetrator.[77] In any case, bringing a variety of backgrounds and voices to the table makes it less likely that board members and managers will support each other unquestioningly on sensitive issues.

Obviously, the larger the company, the more resources can be allocated to anti-corruption programs. But small and mid-sized businesses can do a great deal without spending huge amounts of money or keeping the board or management from other pressing duties. Many free resources are available. Among them are the Organisation for Economic Cooperation and Development (OECD) publication *Corporate Anti-Corruption Compliance Drivers, Mechanisms, and Ideas for Change*,[78] Global Compact Network Canada's *Designing an Anti-Corruption Compliance Program*,[79] and the International Chamber of Commerce's *Business Integrity Compendium*.[80] No matter a firm's size, it can quite easily calibrate its messaging and put in place basic due-diligence procedures. The Canadian Centre of Excellence for Anti-Corruption is an academically based platform geared towards small and mid-sized businesses. It promotes ethical practices and aims to foster collaboration between governments, the private sector, universities, and civil society. Industry-wide codes of conduct are another useful tool, especially if they also apply to suppliers.

Creating a Culture of Integrity

Before developing an anti-corruption compliance program, a company needs to evaluate whether its internal culture in fact encourages honesty and high ethical standards—and, conversely, deters unethical practices. Such a culture has many facets. Leaders need to show that their actions match their words. They need to constantly hammer home the anti-corruption message to staff, including new hires, and that message needs to be integrated into company training programs. Compensation and incentive policies should not encourage employees to think they will be rewarded if they win business through underhanded means. A good audit system is also essential. Auditors can be an effective insurance against situations that management may not otherwise spot.

When evidence of corruption or other abuses does surface, the board must move quickly, starting with a full forensic audit that may need to cover parts of the business beyond where the problem has been identified. If these enquiries confirm wrongdoing, the board should not fall into the trap of automatically trying to hide the problem or to deal with it internally. If criminal acts are suspected, law enforcement authorities should be notified immediately. Meanwhile, the board should pull out the stops to stay ahead of damaging public disclosures with a communications plan, drawn up, if necessary, with the help of outside advisers.

Gerry Tidd, executive vice-president at Australia's Blue-Scope, says success depends on a clear and simple board policy, plus enforcement and training:

> Our people know what our code of business conduct is, what's allowed within it, and what's absolutely not allowed. Sometimes you lose business because of it. In some countries, it's not good business; it's bad business. We don't

mind losing that business, if there's going to be any taint. But we're very clear. The policies are in place, they're trained into people, and they're enforced. We have compliance officers; we have lots of training programs; we have a whistle-blower facility within the company for exactly this sort of stuff. And when we find it, we investigate it thoroughly. And we act.

Claudia Sender, who sits on several European and Brazilian boards, describes how she helped to instill a culture of integrity when she was at the helm of LATAM Airlines:

There were many opportunities where the staff offered me upgrades or things that I wasn't eligible for. And I knew that the moment I accepted them, the word would spread, and others could start taking advantage of the system. But after I said "no" to an upgrade, every time a vice-president or a director of the company would ask for one, the airport agent was very comfortable saying, "Well, not even the CEO is taking upgrades, why am I going to give you one?" So the tone of setting the culture at the top will give people the comfort to do the right thing.

One question that regulatory authorities typically ask and that boards should also bear in mind is how the culture of compliance is measured, whether through surveys, testing, or other means. There is no single method to create and test an effective anti-corruption program. Companies should consider various options, including robust training programs for both employees and external partners, feedback systems, and frequent reassessment of the program. The most effective programs typically include ten key elements:

- Risk assessment to identify areas of potential concern and emphasis

- Clear policies and procedures that lay the foundation for effective controls

- An appropriate tone from the top and messages from middle management

- Supervisory authority assigned to a senior company officer who reports directly to the board or a board committee

- A policy on managing third parties, including due-diligence controls, especially for those deemed at higher risk for corrupt practices

- A hotline and clear guidelines for investigations

- Clear measures for compliance breaches combined with incentives for positive performance

- Periodic testing of the program

- A policy on mergers and acquisitions

- Training and continuing advice

Above all, nurturing an ethical culture demands a questioning mindset, says Export Development Canada president and CEO Mairead Lavery:

> The board and management must continually ask questions. You have to keep up to date because things evolve over time. What was accepted business practice twenty years ago isn't today. And you have to keep questioning ...

Do you have any experience of this? Have you seen this? You have to examine lessons learned when a transaction goes wrong. That's one of the moments that we spend a lot of time on—when something has gone wrong—because then you start to see where your process isn't sufficient to catch a mistake.

How to Investigate

When a concern about corruption is raised, it is common practice for management to notify the board or a board committee. The board then needs to ensure that management thoroughly investigates the matter. There is no universal standard on how to manage and oversee an investigation since the nature of misconduct varies greatly. However, two elements should be paramount: independence and accuracy. For those reasons, the investigation should be carried out either by or with the help of an outside expert, such as a lawyer or forensic auditor, reporting directly to the board. Under no circumstances, should the investigation be handled by the affected employee's supervisor.

The investigating team should create a plan early in the process that spells out rules for capturing and reviewing documents and e-mails, and for talking to potential witnesses. Any cases of fraudulent behaviour must be documented, even if they don't relate to the underlying investigation. Ideally, the investigation will also identify steps to correct any weaknesses in existing processes.

Hernandez advises boards to commission an independent review of their anti-corruption program every year or two:

Most of the sales agent contracts that I've seen over the last twenty years looked solid on paper. They had all the standard anti-corruption clauses, audit rights, and other good things you would expect. But that paper facade of diligence only served to conceal the real truth: the agents were little more than a vehicle to outsource improper payments that company employees could not process themselves. I've seen agents entrusted with multi-million-dollar slush funds to pay for lavish gifts and entertainment, or otherwise divert money to public officials or customers. So, it's important to deeply examine the function of sales agents and other intermediaries operating outside company oversight. From a law enforcement perspective, if your third-party business partners are involved in misconduct on your behalf, it's the same as if your own employees are the ones breaking the law.

Hernandez adds:

As a board member, the more you are told that things are "under control," the more you should be on alert. A small number of reported allegations does not necessarily mean that there is little misconduct occurring in your company. It could indicate that people are afraid to speak up, or that existing controls are insufficient to detect issues. You should focus more on the substance of reported incidents rather than just raw metrics. Ask yourself, "What do these tell us about the company's culture, strategy, and control environment?" Remember that where there's smoke, there's fire.

The Role of Third Parties

When it comes to corruption, the greatest risk to a company is often not the activities of its own employees but rather that of agents, joint-venture partners, subcontractors, and other intermediaries. Indeed, more than three-quarters of enforcement actions regarding bribes involve third parties, as more and more corrupt activities are channelled through intermediaries.[81] Illegal or unethical payments are often disguised as facilitation fees, gifts, entertainment, and even donations and sponsorships. Boards should be aware that, based on recent court cases, the company is liable for those acting on its behalf and thus needs to pay close attention to the activities of third parties. Procedures and controls must be in place to ensure that funds are being spent on their intended purpose, rather than facilitating improper—and unintended—activities. Particular attention should be paid to any intermediary interacting with a government on the company's behalf, or any entity controlled by the government with which the company is doing business.

Competent boards can minimize these risks by ensuring that management includes suppliers, partners, and agents in anti-corruption training programs, and regularly makes them aware of moves to ensure compliance. This is especially important for larger companies, which often become role models for smaller businesses within their orbit. On a more positive note, boards can reduce the temptation to make illicit payments by investing in social, health, training, and other programs in communities where the company operates. In this way, the company is planting the seeds for long-term economic advancement and social stability, and spending its money on projects supported by local communities.

The board has a duty to ask management for a detailed description of plans for combatting bribery and other forms of corruption. It should ask about procedures, as well as about

training and communications from management to staff,
designed to instill an ethical culture. "If I'm on a board, I'm
very interested in metrics," says Jonathan Drimmer, a partner
in the investigations and white-collar defence practice at law
firm Paul Hastings.

> How many people have been trained and for how long? How
> many investigations have been undertaken? How frequently
> is the hotline being used? Testing the system through met-
> rics allows for potential improvements. There's a good bit
> that the board can do from their position to gain comfort
> that things are being handled in an appropriate way.

Transparency

The bar for transparency in corruption cases has risen markedly in recent years, and competent boards would be well
advised to schedule a vigorous discussion of the issue and
put some clear guidelines in place. Not long ago, boards
were reticent about sharing any news of corruption allegations and subsequent investigations on the grounds that
these were matters best dealt with internally and kept under
wraps. However, perceptive business leaders are realizing
that transparency can, in fact, pay off. Local communities
appreciate openness from companies doing business in their
midst. Likewise, while investors expect a strong financial
performance, they also realize how a bribery scandal can
tarnish a company's reputation and its stock price (see the
case study below), not to mention siphon off funds that
might otherwise be used to pay dividends. In many cases,
transparency can open rather than close doors. Huguette

Labelle, who chairs the International Anti-Corruption Conference, cites the example of a Norwegian company that was asked to pay a bribe in return for a contract in north Africa. The company responded that Norwegian law required it to publish all payments to outsiders. That was the end of any suggestion of a bribe, and the company still landed the contract.

Transparency is also critical in setting the rules for appropriate behaviour, so that employees and suppliers are under no illusion of the consequences of unethical or illegal actions. Claudia Sender describes the "consequence matrix" adopted by some of the companies that she has worked with:

> If you have done one thing wrong, we will educate you, and we will give you training. The second time, you will be suspended. Third strike, and you're out. The consequences of wrongdoing should be very dire and clear to people. You can define how harsh you want your compliance consequence matrix to be. But once it's defined, it has to be applied with no exceptions, and with a special focus on leaders.

Tough Choices

Rooting out corruption may seem like a straightforward case of right versus wrong, but it can also raise some difficult issues for the board and senior management. A company may have been paying bribes for years to government officials who facilitate a long-standing contract. Employees may be under heavy pressure to make an improper payment in order to meet their sales targets or to win over an important new customer. The misbehaviour may amount to no more than a few notes stuffed into the hand of a customs official to ensure that a shipment reaches its destination on time. Or it can be as seemingly insignificant or irrelevant as employees who hand loose change to a traffic officer just so they can reach an important business appointment on time.

The board and management face tough choices in dealing with issues such as these, and the consequences need to be carefully considered. For example, what message is sent to employees if a jolly farewell party is held for a long-serving executive who is "retiring" but is in fact being quietly terminated for unethical or corrupt behaviour? By the same token, what threats to personal safety might a faraway employee or contractor and their families face if improper payments to a corrupt government official are suddenly revealed and ended? Just how much information should the company provide to law enforcement authorities, shareholders, and others?

Jonathan Drimmer describes the bind that boards risk finding themselves in if they follow the seemingly easy and tempting path:

> Once you make one payment, you are on the hook forever. They will keep coming back and coming back, and you will never get out from under it. It also really undermines the security of your title, of your tenure, of your situation. Because at any given point, if you're making a facilitating payment to get a contract or a licence or a permit, the government can come back and say, "Hey, this was issued in an improper way," and ultimately take away what you thought you had lawfully. So it is always a good idea to be prepared to walk away if you have to, and to think in terms of the long game, as opposed to just getting something done

quickly and easily, and inviting the parade of challenges that comes when you start making payments that aren't proper.

Preparation is key to avoiding such situations, and boards need to be comfortable with those preparations. In many cases, the ethical path may cost the company a substantial amount of business, at least in the short term. Even so, a competent board must take a clear stand and look beyond the immediate benefits. It needs to issue unambiguous directives such as: We do not bribe government officials. We do not pay money to get inside information to win a deal. There will be no double standards and no exceptions, including (perhaps especially) for star performers. Perhaps most crucially, the board and management must assure employees and contractors that the company will stand behind them if they lose a deal because they refuse to pay a bribe. As with so many other ESG issues, the company's long-term reputation and sustainability are always paramount.

CASE STUDY: SNC-LAVALIN

When it comes to corruption, few companies anywhere in the world have had a more humbling experience than SNC-Lavalin (SNC), the Montreal-based engineering and construction group. The company has been battered by allegations of wrongdoing involving contracts in Libya, Bangladesh, Cambodia, Mozambique, and Uganda, among others. In 2019, it admitted paying CA$127 million in bribes to Libyan officials between 2001 and 2011 to secure contracts in that country. About a third of the funds went to the son of Muammar Gaddafi, the former Libyan leader. A Canadian court fined the company CA$280 million, to be paid over five years. A Quebec jury also found a former SNC executive guilty on charges of fraud, corruption of foreign officials, and money laundering.

Since the corruption allegations surfaced, the board has left few stones unturned in an effort to rehabilitate SNC's reputation. Among the measures taken over an eight-year period:

- The board hired an external expert to investigate a whistle-blower's allegations of a corrupt CA$56 million payment to an agent. It disclosed the outcome of the probe, and a Swiss court convicted a former SNC employee.

- The company has signed settlement agreements with the World Bank, the Canadian government, and the African Development Bank. The World Bank barred SNC from doing business with it for ten years and demanded that it put a robust compliance program in place. However, it granted an early release in April 2021, after only eight years. A World Bank monitor visited three or four SNC sites per year in different locations around the world to examine its new compliance procedures. As part of the African Development Bank settlement, SNC contributed to an outreach fund.

- In April 2012, the company invited Siemens's chief executive to address senior management on how the

German electrical engineering group transformed itself in the wake of a 2008 corruption and bribery scandal. (Coincidentally, the police raided SNC's offices in Montreal on the same day in 2012 that the Siemens group was there.)

- SNC hired the Ethisphere Institute, an Arizona-based company that defines and measures corporate ethical standards, to certify its new anti-corruption program. The certification was renewed in 2020 for another two years.

- It set up a compliance investigations team, at one time comprising twenty-five employees, to review every one of the company's projects. "We really made sure that we understood whether there were any more issues out there," says Hentie Dirker, whom SNC recruited from Siemens in 2015 as its chief integrity officer.

- It has implemented a new organizational structure, including the appointment of several compliance officers, and has adopted anti-corruption procedures based on global best practices.

- It has set up an external whistle-blowing line for outsiders as well as employees. A small committee reviews calls received each week and refers them to the appropriate division of the company for further investigation.

As Dirker sees it, one of the most effective weapons to counter corruption is to hold individuals accountable for their misdeeds:

It's not a company that's corrupt. It's not a company that commits fraud or bribery. It is individuals or people within the company that do that. So a company should work together with law enforcement, give them all the necessary information that allows them to go after those individuals. It should look at whether the programs are robust enough and, if not, to make them better.

(For the latest information, see **https://www. snclavalin.com/en/about/integrity**)

■■■

Guidelines for Competent Boards

» Build a culture of honesty and transparency.

» Assure employees and contractors that the company will stand behind them if they lose a deal after refusing to pay a bribe.

» Ensure that at least one member of the board is familiar with anti-corruption processes and provide suitable training for all board members.

» Be counterintuitive. If everything seems to be going right, dig deeper. Ask probing questions of top performers.

» Keep questioning management about the effectiveness of anti-corruption measures to ensure you are fulfilling your fiduciary obligations.

» Vet all intermediaries in business deals carefully, especially those who have dealings with government officials.

» Appoint independent third parties to conduct corruption investigations and audits of company procedures.

» Anticipate new forms of corruption involving, for example, cybercrime, dark money, and misuse of private and public goods.

Ten Key Questions

(Recommended exercise: Ask each director to answer these questions independently. Then compare and discuss. More details on page 231.)

1. What are the main risks that your company faces from corruption and lack of transparency?
2. Which board members have the expertise to exercise oversight on corruption, integrity, and transparency issues?
3. What is the board doing to instill a culture that mitigates those risks?
4. Does your company have anti-corruption policies and procedures to prevent and detect bribery? Does every employee know the rules? How does the board oversee these policies?
5. Do these rules cover the following: facilitation payments, per diems, political contributions, sponsorships and charitable donations, government-related meals, gifts, entertainment, travel, lobbying expenses through industry associations and other third-party organizations?

6. Does your company have a conflicts-of-interest policy? When did the board last review and update it?

7. Does a senior officer have specific responsibility to oversee anti-corruption efforts, with a direct reporting line to the board?

8. Are anti-corruption programs subject to regular audits to test their effectiveness? How often does the board discuss the management of anti-corruption risks and key performance indicators to ensure they are effective?

9. Is there a way for employees and third parties to report corruption concerns anonymously and safely?

10. Is your company sufficiently transparent about its anti-corruption program?

REFLECTIONS

"It's important to push and develop a corporate culture where everyone feels responsible and accountable. Officers, managers, and employees can question the integrity of business decisions and whether they are truly aligned with corporate interests and not personal interests."

–Iohann Le Frapper, vice-chair, International Chamber of Commerce Corporate Responsibility and Anti-corruption International Commission

CHAPTER 8

Data: It's About Risk, Not Technology

"Never get tired of this, because it's just not going to go away."

–Bojana Bellamy, president, Centre for Information
Policy Leadership

WHY THIS MATTERS

The Economist proclaimed in a May 2017 headline: THE WORLD'S MOST VALUABLE RESOURCE IS NO LONGER OIL, BUT DATA. For good reason. Smartphones and the Internet have made data abundant, ubiquitous, and extremely valuable. Whether we are taking a walk, watching TV, or just sitting in traffic, virtually every human activity these days leaves a digital mark that any number of players can potentially use for good or ill. The volume of these digital footprints is mushrooming as more and more devices—from watches to cars to home security systems—are connected to the Internet. According to one estimate, a self-driving car will generate 100 gigabytes of data per second. But the growing importance of data comes not only from its volume. Cutting-edge artificial intelligence (AI) techniques, such as machine learning, can extract enormous value from it. Algorithms can predict when a customer is ready to buy, when a jet engine needs servicing, or when a person is most at risk from various diseases. On the flip side, however, the collection and use of big data raise thorny issues that reach deep into almost every facet of our society—privacy, crime, equity, sustainability, accessibility, competition policy … to name a few.

Since much of the world's data is created, used, and stored by businesses, every competent board needs to pay as close attention to the organization's data policies as to its financial statements or sustainability goals. On one hand, data can be an invaluable asset, helping companies to offer customers what they want and to refine their marketing strategies to the nth degree. It can become a revenue stream if a company chooses to sell data obtained from customers to data brokers and advertising agencies. The use of AI and machine learning can sharpen a company's competitive advantage, while data management policies in general can become a business differentiator, separating the efficient from the less productive. Handled properly, data can help a company burnish its reputation, letting customers and suppliers know that its brand protects them better than anyone else's brand, that it has gone above and beyond a minimum standard, and that it is aiming to be the standard-bearer in its sector. However, none of the benefits that data offers can be fully realized without a company—including the board—taking account of some serious and far-reaching risks and ethical dilemmas.

High on the list of risks is a cyberattack. While most attacks are small in scale and quickly resolved, some have proven devastating to companies in terms of both cost and reputation. A notable example was the theft of the personal information of almost 150 million people from the credit monitoring company Equifax in 2017. US regulators ended up fining Atlanta-based Equifax US$700 million, and Moody's lowered its outlook on the company's debt from stable to negative, the first time that a cyberattack had affected a company's credit rating. A 2017 Ponemon Institute survey estimated that almost two-thirds of data breach victims lost trust in an organization because of the breach.[82] What's more, according to a 2020 study by FTI Consulting, companies steeled themselves for a 9 percent drop in global annual revenue in the event of a data privacy crisis.[83]

Boards can also no longer afford to overlook the ethical implications of their data policies. Take the algorithms used for AI, which may promote a product and boost a company's profit, but could also eliminate choice for its customers because they are prevented from seeing other options available to them. "It's so easy to become blinded by the amazing capabilities of targeting people in groups and really dissecting that demographic to what you want," observes Tyson Johnson, CEO of CyberNB, a Canadian cybersecurity non-profit. "But remember that it can also be used on the flip side."

Dottie Schindlinger, executive director of the Diligent Institute, the governance think tank and research arm of Diligent Corporation, observes that "cyber-risk plays a huge role in board conversations. It has become one of the top topics happening around board tables over the last couple of years. We are watching so many companies that really pride themselves on having this impenetrable architecture being brought to their knees by cyberattackers." However, in a caveat worthy of note by every board, Schindlinger adds:

We're not judging companies so harshly on whether or not they have been breached, but on how well they respond afterwards. How quickly they react. Are they prepared? Have they had drills? Have they had tabletop exercises at the leadership level? What level of prowess does the board and leadership have in terms of understanding the full scope of the breach, and how to respond and react to it? Those are the things that actually matter now.

How to Prepare

While data can dramatically improve business productivity, companies must act as stewards rather than owners of this crucial asset. For boards, that means putting some guardrails in place to ensure that data under their control is used only for the purposes for which it was designed. Because regulatory and legal frameworks cannot keep pace with rapidly changing technologies, the onus falls on the board and management to weigh the risks and consequences of using technologies such as AI and machine learning. Data privacy, transparency, interpretability, integrity, control, and accountability should all be part of such assessments.

A good place for board members to start is by reading the 2017 Montreal Declaration for a Responsible Development of Artificial Intelligence, which aims to spark public debate and encourage the progressive and inclusive development of AI. Every director should also be familiar with the European Union's far-reaching General Data Protection Regulation, implemented in 2018. Widely known as GDPR and viewed as a pioneer in data protection and privacy, this regulation is making its influence felt well beyond EU member states. Several other countries and states, including Brazil, China, California, Japan, India, Russia, and South Africa, either have adopted or are in the process of adopting similar measures.[84] Given GDPR's growing impact, every board should consider the extent to which its company is in compliance with the regulation, and what can be done to improve compliance. Those inclined to dismiss GDPR as unimportant or irrelevant may wish to consider the advice of Kersi Porbunderwalla, president and CEO of the e-Compliance Academy: "If you think compliance is expensive, I suggest you try non-compliance," he says. "That is really going to be expensive when it comes to money and reputation."

Once a board is familiar with the overall landscape of data management and cybersecurity, Lisa Reshaur, Microsoft's general manager for digital security and resilience, suggests the following steps:

> Start with understanding the strategy. Understand your top risks. Make sure you're clear on what the company isn't focused on. Understand what incidents it has had in the past and how it's handled them, and then understand what, if any, role the board would have if there were major cyber incidents. And what you would need to know if someone in the company was to pick up the phone and call you. What are they looking for from you?

A competent board and executive team should keep asking themselves tough questions about data management. Should the company be collecting and using certain kinds of data just because it has access to it? How long should it be keeping the data? Does it have proper consent from customers and others? What is being gained from the data that the company is using? Can those benefits be quantified? And so on. Tamara Somers, senior specialist at Telstra's sustainability centre of excellence, describes the Australian telecom company's approach to these issues as follows:

> One of the things that we put to our board and to our management team was that it was really important to define for ourselves what best practice looked like, drawing on emerging trends around the world. We couldn't wait for governments to catch up and regulate the space. We needed to make our own decisions, using our own moral compass about what we wouldn't do as an organization, what kinds of technologies we were prepared to use, and how we were going to do that. We would also seek to work collectively with like-minded businesses and with governments in all the jurisdictions where we operate to get some kind of global alignment on standards. The key role for directors in this space is to set the tone of the conversation that should happen in the organization.

It is all too tempting for a board to think of cybersecurity and data management as matters best left to the IT and legal departments. Nothing could be further from the truth. As Chris Crummey of IBM's centre for government cybersecurity puts it: "Cybersecurity is one thousand percent about risk. Stakeholders need to have risk-based business discussions. Mature customers look at cybersecurity as a business challenge, and not just about technology. You can see it in their 'security culture' and how they are organized internally."

While technical proficiency and legal compliance are critical, data management also raises important issues related to trust, privacy, growth, and, indeed, overall business strategy. It is thus vital for the board to encourage an integrated approach that involves every part of the company and every employee, including board members themselves.

Part of that approach means having a technology team in place that can communicate effectively with the board, bearing in mind that tech specialists typically come from a younger generation than board members, and tend to speak a different language. As I have pointed out in other contexts, the composition of the board and senior management needs to be sufficiently diverse to facilitate communication with younger staff members with specific specialties. Porbunderwalla observes:

> Probably most boards have the competencies that can address the legal issues. But we need to make sure that a person on the board also understands technology. Otherwise, the legal person is going to override the technology person, and that is not the right approach. You need to make sure that they speak the same language and are able to allocate the resources in the right way.

Riding the Digital Revolution

Every competent board needs to know how the company plans to adapt to the next generation of data management or digitization. Its top priority should be to familiarize itself with emerging 5G technology, which is set to revolutionize data communication over the next few years in terms of speed, quantity, and capability. Processes that currently take minutes to complete will be done in seconds. "If you think that you're dealing with big data today, multiply it by forty and that will be the amount of data that you have in your organization," says Porbunderwalla. 5G is expected to enable companies to make far greater use of AI, data profiling, and general digitization as everything is connected. Those that seize the opportunity will have a distinct competitive advantage; those that fail to do so face the risk of falling by the wayside. Worse, the laggards could open the way to cyber-criminals. Given the shortage of IT specialists around the world, in-house training could be crucial.

Boards need to be aware, however, that digitization does not come cheap and that there is no such thing as cheap data. That applies to every facet of a data overhaul, starting with having properly trained experts, to installation of new systems, and, finally, to compliance with an emerging array of government regulations covering cybersecurity and privacy. Any board that seeks to cut corners on cost could end up paying dearly in the form of data breaches, penalties, and lost business opportunities. Boards should especially avoid the temptation of trying to layer new systems and controls on top of existing ones. Instead, they should lean towards an appropriate long-term investment in the most up-to-date technology. Porbunderwalla has a special word of advice for small companies: "Make sure that even though you are small, you think big. Think big data, think data transformation, think data structures so that you don't get hit by cybercriminals or the oversight authorities because you are non-compliant." Failing to do the job properly could also make it difficult to obtain suitable insurance coverage for data breaches and other catastrophic events.

Some other tips for boards to follow as the digital revolution gathers momentum:

- Identify three key vulnerabilities in the company's current systems, address those, and then move on to others.

- Make sure you have the right people, the right systems, and the right structure to implement proper cybersecurity systems.

- Get legal advice on the board's liability for IT and cybersecurity. As Porbunderwalla puts it: "I can assure you, if the board is liable, if the chair of the board is going to prison, he is going to make sure that all controls and all implementations are done the right way."

- Ensure that your organization's culture is geared to discipline, appropriate controls, and accountability.

- Focus on three words: integration, embedding, and automation. Controls can be automated only if every IT component is integrated into the overall system.

- Ensure that digitization projects comply with official policies and regulations from the start, and that this compliance is thoroughly documented. "Digital transformation is not re-engineering," Porbunderwalla notes. "If you have to re-engineer as part of your digitization, you're on the wrong track. Digitization is achieving compliance by design."

Culture Matters

Experts agree that the key to robust data management is to weave security into the fabric of the corporate culture. Competent boards should be setting the tone and driving the conversations that lead to such an outcome. This is especially true in smaller companies that cannot afford teams of cyber-security experts, and where the example set by individuals is likely to have a greater impact than reams of policies and procedures. The board should keep asking whether its policies pass the so-called "sunshine" test, in other words, whether board members would feel comfortable if they saw a media report describing the company's technology and its approach to cybersecurity.

Transparency is generally a big part of this equation. In the case of AI, for example, employees and customers should be aware of what data is being collected, how it is being used, and how that use may affect them. Somers says that "in some cases, we've made the judgment call that customers are not ready for us to use that kind of data or are not willing for us to use certain types of information, and therefore we should hold off using those technologies." She adds:

> It's really critical for boards to understand that although there may not be laws relating to AI at the moment, existing laws do apply. For example, if you have an anti-discrimination law in the jurisdictions where you operate, then that applies regardless of whether it's a machine or a human making the decision.

PROTECTING BOARD MEMBERS' DATA

Directors often sit on multiple boards, have numerous other outside interests, and use multiple e-mail addresses. A company thus faces a daunting challenge to ensure that board members' communications are secure and not compromising the corporate data and other assets. Lisa Reshaur, Microsoft's general manager for digital security and resilience, advises all board members to ask themselves a few simple questions:

- Do I change my password regularly?
- Is it a complex password?
- Do I have two-factor authentication turned on?
- Have I partitioned my networks so that my family communications and household devices are walled off from my board work?
- Have I considered hiring an expert to set up these separate networks at home or to assess what has been set up?

The Wild West of Fake News

Whether we like it or not, misinformation and fake news have become a fact of modern life and, as such, can pose a headache for boards and management, and even a threat to a company's business. In years gone by, consumers of news would typically read several newspapers and magazines, and watch or listen to news from a handful of trusted sources, enabling them to weigh up different points of view. By the same token, media outlets typically went to great lengths to ensure that their reporting was accurate and fair. Life is no longer so simple. Mainstream publications and TV networks have lost ground to an array of other news sources, some trying to maintain a modicum of accuracy and fairness, but a multitude of others peddling fake news, rumours, doctored pictures, propaganda, and conspiracy theories. For many citizens, social media has become the only source of news, putting them at the mercy of algorithms and those with the loudest voices.

A competent board would be wise to view misinformation as a significant risk and to put protective countermeasures in place, just as it would for any other risk. These include responsibility for monitoring social media, and what to do when potentially harmful misinformation strikes. The traditional response of threatening legal action may have little impact in an environment where misinformation can go viral in a matter of hours or even minutes, doing severe damage to a company's reputation before anyone has a chance to respond. Advance preparation and watchfulness are key so that the damage can be minimized quickly and forcefully.

If the company has been able to win stakeholders' trust in the past through effective communication and engagement, that reputation should shield it from the worst excesses of misinformation. A high level of trust means that employees, shareholders, customers, and suppliers will give the company the benefit of the doubt before they rush down the rabbit hole of "can you believe that company XYZ did this?" But to reach that point, a company should be prepared for an onslaught that would have seemed unimaginable in days gone by. Done right and with a bit of luck, the reaction of outsiders when fake news strikes will not be, "Oh gosh, what a terrible company that is," but rather, "Is that really true? Could it perhaps be fake? Let me make the company aware of this."

Privacy

How companies use the data they collect has become a matter of vigorous public debate and, increasingly, public policy and regulation. So much so that governments are looking for ways to set more stringent limits on data use in order to protect individual privacy. Boards need to be familiar with these developments. Laws such as the EU's General Data Protection Regulation and, to a lesser extent, California's Consumer Privacy Act require boards to maintain records showing that they have signed off on policies related to data privacy, such as retention of records, consent procedures, and maintaining data quality. More than that, a board can expect to be held accountable for a data breach or theft of company records that compromises the privacy of employees or customers.

The moves towards greater accountability are encouraging a fresh approach to data privacy, with boards asking many more questions about their company's data management policies. Many companies are reconsidering what data they should collect, and how to use it. They are embedding privacy protections into the design of new products and services, and ensuring that everyone in the company, from engineers to the human resources and marketing departments, understands the importance of privacy and works together to set up effective and ethical processes. The most progressive players are also reaching out to stakeholders on issues related to data privacy and working to publicize their data policies more coherently so that customers know what they are signing up for. Corporate policies that take account of privacy, security, and transparency issues can go a long way towards building trust with stakeholders and regulators.

Lessons from COVID

One legacy of the COVID-19 pandemic has been an explosion in the use of data—and the dilemmas it creates. The volume of data traffic is higher than ever before. Working from home has brought enormous new challenges for organizations of all kinds in terms of access to data, protection of data, and accountability. At the same time, the surge of online shopping and banking has given businesses access to vast new troves of personal data, but also exposed them and their customers to new threats from hackers and other criminals. The pandemic is causing a reassessment of many other data-related issues, such as the extent to which employees should be monitored at home, and the protection of data in unfamiliar surroundings.

With a company's reputation depending more than ever on how it manages and protects its data, a competent board dare not ignore these trends. In a sign of the times, IBM's Crummey has noticed that many customers are starting to adopt a zero-trust strategy, not only internally but also with their supply chain. "Risk-based adaptive access allows a company to 'never trust, always verify' as it weaves security around every user, all devices, and every connection continuously," he says. "Focusing on making this implementation frictionless for the human is key to success. This is a key foundation for a lot of mature cybersecurity strategies."

CASE STUDY: VANCOUVER CITY SAVINGS CREDIT UNION (VANCITY)

Vancity, Canada's largest credit union, had the misfortune of suffering a failure of its entire online banking operation on the Thursday before the Thanksgiving weekend in October 2018. The outage continued for most of the long weekend, raising fears that ranged from a massive data breach to the ability of customers to withdraw urgently needed funds. Anita Braha, Vancity's chair, recalls how she and her fellow board members navigated one of the most challenging times in the credit union's history:

> During those few days, I was on the phone with our (then) CEO Tamara Vrooman every hour or two from early in the morning until about ten or eleven o'clock at night. I tried to make sure I understood what was happening, at the same time trying to make decisions and determinations in real time about how best to support Tamara. And how best to make sure that we as a board were doing our job.
>
> In one of the first calls with Tamara, I said that I saw my role at this critical time as an extra set

of eyes and ears and thoughts: "Just to make sure that I'm relaying to you what I think are important things for us to consider, to be a sounding board for you and to be supportive so that we get through this in as robust and appropriate a manner as possible." The second thing I said to her was that we needed to think about our members, from the single member who may need access to their banking information online all the way to the larger members who may be buying or selling a home, or buying or selling businesses or cars, or needing loans.

Tamara told me that we were reaching out through the branches to members who we know have transactions that need to be conducted today and tomorrow. And we were literally writing cheques, like in the old days, and couriering them to lawyers' offices to make sure that we were able to meet our members' needs. We kept our branches open throughout the entire long weekend. We also did extensive communications on social media, and Tamara did a number of interviews to keep our members apprised in real time as to what was happening.

On the back end of things, Tamara and I spoke at the very beginning about who we need to keep apprised. Obviously, the board members. Also our regulator, up to and including government ministers, if appropriate, and fellow stakeholders in the credit union system, to make sure that we were canvassing all of our responsibilities.

The other part of this for me as chair was how to make sure that I was keeping my board colleagues apprised. I would send e-mails during the day, and I did speak with my vice-chair, including discussing whether to call a board meeting. I took the decision late in the day on Friday that I would call a board meeting. The difficulty was that it was unscheduled, and it was the long weekend. We had the call on the Saturday because of the need to give people notice and the ability to make sure they were able to call in. We had our chief technical officer and others apprise the board of the situation. A couple of things came out of that. One was that the board was very keen to stay connected and engaged. I said I wanted to call a further extraordinary board meeting for the Sunday in Vancouver, in person, if people were able to make it. To a person, they all attended.

During that second meeting, the board indicated that they wanted me as chair to speak to the membership directly via a video. And so I did that. One thing that we wanted to do was to repeatedly assure our members that there was no breach of their data, and that their financial assets were secure. They also wanted me to tell the membership that the board was on top of the issue and was regularly being kept informed, and that we would commission an independent third-party review of what had taken place, and report to the membership when we had that information.

Rather than closing down, we opened up and reached out to our members. And I can say proudly that, as far as I'm aware, we didn't lose a member. In fact, over those few days, we gained a few members. There were a lot of very touching moments of members coming into branches, bringing cookies and treats for the staff because they were so appreciative.

But it's not something I'd recommend that one go through. It really tested us and showed that our values were able to come to the fore at a time of crisis. Of course, we had business continuity policies and incident response policies, but as we all know, things rarely happen the way they're scripted in the manual. This is where your character and your judgment come into play. As chair, I believed it was critical for me to have developed a very strong working relationship with my CEO. I remember saying to her, at the beginning of our working relationship, that if and when a crisis occurred, we would need a lot of trust and credibility and respect between us. I think that was demonstrated during that time.

The other part of your responsibility as chair is to develop relationships with your board colleagues. What we did as a board together is a testament to the kind of collegiality we had built, because there are times when you need to make decisions quickly, and you need to have confidence that the person that you're dealing with is a person of integrity, a person of substance, and someone who has a clear sense of where we need to be going. A whole other aspect was our relationship with our regulator. Because we had a good, strong relationship, the regulator allowed us to do our work, including the third-party review. It's not glamorous work, all this preparation, all this ground building. But it sure is nice to be able to rely on it in times of crisis.

The fact that I am a lawyer was a benefit to me, but it's important to have a broad variety of skills and attributes at the table. Another director, who had a wealth of experience in the political realm, pointed out that we needed to do more as a board to reach out to the membership. I could say I wished that we had someone with in-depth knowledge of technology. It may have made our response even better. But at the end of the day, the CEO was engaged in trying to determine what happened. Our chief technical officer was fantastic in the depth of his knowledge and his ability to present the board. I'm of the view that our job is to govern, not to delve into the detail. You rely on good judgment, good character, and an ability to stay composed and calm during a crisis. You set the tone from the top. I was very clear about what my role was, which was not to attack our CEO, not to blame her, but to support her through this crisis and to be as present as I could be.

Guidelines for Competent Boards

» Emphasize that cybersecurity and responsible use of data is everyone's duty. Policies, procedures, and controls should be integrated across the entire company.

» Be sure that the company can immediately detect a cybersecurity breach and has processes and detailed plans in place to ensure minimal disruption to day-to-day business.

» Don't collect data you don't need. And don't keep it for too long. If the data is obsolete after a year, destroy it.

» Use the resources of trade and industry associations (especially small companies).

» Include due diligence on data privacy and data security in any mergers or acquisitions.

» Always bear in mind the ethical issues associated with big data, collection of personal information, and artificial intelligence.

» Keep asking whether your company can use its data to unlock new business opportunities.

Ten Key Questions

(Recommended exercise: Ask each director to answer these questions independently. Then compare and discuss. More details on page 231.)

1. Does the company have overarching cybersecurity and data privacy policies? Who oversees, enforces, and is accountable for them?

2. When did board members last read the policies that the company asks its digital users to approve? Did you fully understand them? Do you think your customers fully understand them?

3. Are all board members familiar with terms such as ransomware, DDOS, and phishing attacks? More generally, which board members have the expertise to exercise oversight on cybersecurity and data issues?

4. How often does the board receive training and adequate updates on cybersecurity, IT, responsible use of data, and digital trends?

5. Do the company's cybersecurity and data use policies align with its business priorities, including its ESG strategy?

6. Who is responsible for overseeing the ethical aspects of data management?

7. Is the company able to document its compliance with regulatory requirements regarding data management and privacy?

8. Can the company ensure timely detection of a cyberattack or data breach? Have detailed plans been drawn up to deal with such a catastrophic event?

9. Does the company have sufficient insurance to cover the full damage from a cyberattack?

10. Does the board understand the ways in which 5G technology may impact the business, employees, customers, and other stakeholders?

REFLECTIONS

"Don't collect data you don't need. And don't keep it too long. If the data is obsolete, destroy it, don't keep it in your backup. This is one way to start adopting the principles of 'privacy by design.'"

–Josée Morin, human resources and governance committee chair, CIMA+; cybersecurity and digital transformation expert

"Privacy and security are very important topics that we are relentlessly putting effort and work into to make sure that both we and our customers are as safe as possible."

–Hans Koeleman, former chief, corporate communications and corporate social responsibility, KPN

CHAPTER 9

Paying Our Dues

"As a director, your duty first and foremost is to ensure the
 long-term success of the business. And that means balancing
 being a good citizen with making sure that you take care of
 the interests of the shareholders, as well as the stakeholders."

*–Birgit Noergaard, director of DSV and
 numerous other international companies*

WHY THIS MATTERS

Until quite recently, directors felt free to oversee their company's financial affairs with little regard for the views of
outsiders. But that attitude is under intensifying scrutiny as
investors, regulators, advocacy groups, and even the public at
large ask whether businesses are using their resources not just
to produce maximum profit and boost the share price but also
for the greater good. This chapter considers this shift from
the standpoint of three financial issues that appear on almost
every board agenda and are attracting ever more public attention: taxation, executive pay, and long-term investments.

Companies have traditionally pulled out the stops to pay
as little tax as possible within the confines of the law. Taking
maximum advantage of tax loopholes and tax havens has been
a source of pride, even if it means that a hugely profitable

business ends up paying not a single cent in taxes. Such tax avoidance has become even more prevalent with the growth of the digital economy, which makes it more difficult for governments to tax many transactions. But while tax avoidance may be quite legal, it now tends to draw more disdain than admiration in many quarters. Pointing to the critical public services funded by taxes, critics argue that every business ought to pay its fair share, and that using legal loopholes to avoid doing so is unethical and contrary to the spirit of tax policy. The Organisation for Economic Co-operation and Development (OECD) estimates that tax loopholes cost governments worldwide between 4 percent and 10 percent of global corporate income tax revenues, equal to a revenue loss of US$100 billion to US$240 billion.[85] Every time a company finds a loophole that enables it to pay less tax, it is forcing a government to find that revenue elsewhere, with much of the burden being pushed onto workers through higher personal income taxes. Ethics is also permeating the issue of executive pay, the second issue that boards must tackle in a very different way these days. In one of the landmark corporate governance developments over the past few decades, shareholders are increasingly demanding a "say on pay" to rein in egregiously unfair compensation practices. Indeed, excessive compensation has become one of the main reasons for shareholders ousting executives and directors in proxy votes. Securities regulators are also paying closer attention to pay practices and mandating more transparency. Shai Ganu, head of Willis Towers Watson's global executive compensation and board governance practice, says that "stakeholders, clients, and companies are definitely asking for management teams to be held accountable for the impact they have on society at large. More and more companies are asking us and asking themselves: 'How do we incorporate broader stakeholder measures into good executive compensation plans?'" Executive pay deemed excessive or misaligned with stakeholders' interests, Ganu says, "may cause reputational damage, because it makes constituents—including your employees, clients, and supply-chain partners—feel that you don't really care about the broader community and you don't really care about them. All you're interested in is squeezing every last dollar and maximizing short-term returns, compromising longer-term sustainability."

Finally, competent boards need to bring a fresh mindset to capital investment. Thinking about the company's own long-term outlook is no longer enough; instead, boards must consider what the world around them will look like in five, ten, and even fifty years' time—and it is sure to be a very different world from the one we live in today. Volatile weather, higher sea levels, and the many other consequences of climate change will have a big impact on the type of infrastructure that companies use. Boards should also be asking how to accommodate emerging workplace trends such as remote work and advances in digital technology. Will office buildings still be needed? How will building regulations adjust to the greater likelihood of extreme weather events? How will people and goods be transported? What manufacturing processes will be overtaken by 3-D printing? What kind of building materials will be favoured in 2050? Which assets will insurance companies be willing to cover as the climate becomes more unpredictable? These are some of the questions that could dramatically affect investment plans over the next few decades.

A sign of the times is the agreement by 130 countries in early July 2021 to back a global minimum corporate tax rate of at least 15 percent. The deal aims to end what US Treasury Secretary Janet Yellen has called "a thirty-year race to the bottom on corporate tax rates" and includes plans to prevent tech giants and other multinationals from shifting profits into tax havens. The agreement is a long-overdue recognition that if a company establishes itself in a country, it needs to pay its dues. It is no longer acceptable in the court of public opinion to pay a pittance—or indeed nothing—in taxes and then argue that you are simply following the rules and have nothing to be ashamed of.

The G7 accord is just one of a slew of initiatives driving home the message that businesses have an obligation to constituencies beyond their shareholders. Elsewhere, the United Nations has identified tax policy as playing a vital role in achieving its sustainable development goals. The OECD is spearheading talks among 140 countries on rules for taxing cross-border digital services and curbing tax-base erosion. In 2019, Amsterdam-based Global Reporting Initiative published the first global reporting standard that combines management disclosures on tax strategy with public country-by-country reporting of business activities, revenues, profit, and tax. Known as GRI 207, the standard aims to help organizations become more transparent in their financial reporting and, in the process, improve policy-making, investment decisions, and business sustainability. "It is the first time that an international standard setter is putting forward a disclosure standard on tax payments to governments," says Timothy Mohin, GRI's former chief executive and former senior director of corporate responsibility at Advanced Micro Devices. "Why does that matter? Because companies have to pay their fair share. Increasingly, stakeholders are of the perception that they are not paying their fair share, and so there has been an outcry for more transparency on what companies are actually paying in the places they do business."

Similar pressures are coming to the fore on issues related to executive pay and capital investment. According to a 2021 Willis Towers Watson report, executive incentive plans include some form of ESG component at 63 percent of companies included in Europe's major stock-market indices, 52 percent of S&P 500 companies, and 68 percent of companies making up the Toronto stock exchange's TSX 60 index.[86] When it comes to long-term investment, boards are being challenged to consider events and consequences that have never before been on their radar, such as the heightened risk of impaired or stranded assets, described in more detail below.

How to Prepare

At a time when corporate policies and actions are being watched more closely than ever, a competent board needs to understand how to integrate broad socio-economic factors into its assessment of business performance. By doing so, it can drive closer collaboration among key stakeholders, both within and outside the company, leading to more informed, transparent, and widely accepted decisions.

One of the toughest challenges facing board members in this regard is the inevitable trade-offs involved in issues such as taxation, long-term investments, and executive compensation. To take just one example, if a company's business model is to offer customers bargain-basement prices, that may be good for the customers and for shareholders, but could also mean that the company is paying unacceptably low wages or not spending enough on health and safety measures. As pointed out throughout this book, enlightened corporate governance now requires directors to consider the benefits and costs of their decisions not only for shareholders but also for the many other constituencies that make up the community to which the company belongs. Recognizing that obligation is a critical first step towards finding a fair solution. Barbara Oberleitner, global head of tax and special projects at engineering consultancy WSP, says that, at her company, "we're always questioning ourselves and considering the reputational risk when we make a decision from a tax perspective."

Ethical Tax

Businesses have traditionally rushed to take advantage of any scheme or loophole that might lower their tax bill and produce a fatter profit. Over the past five years or so, however, investors have started pushing back against this approach on the grounds that a relentless drive to pay less tax ignores a company's wider responsibility to society and ends up doing more harm than good. Compliance with the law is turning out to be only part of the duties expected from a competent board. It also needs to consider the wider implications of tax avoidance. That requires a marked shift in culture within most companies, given that tax specialists have up to now been trained to focus on the possible and the legal, rather than the ethical.

Mia d'Adhemar, senior manager at Global Reporting Initiative, says that two of the questions her organization asks are: How is the approach to tax linked to the business and sustainable development strategies of the organization? Might you be making commitments in your sustainable development strategy that you're not living up to in your approach to tax? "Those are the sorts of questions that board members could perhaps be looking at," d'Adhemar notes. "If they're not doing so yet, organizations should be expecting questions from large investors on this topic. And it won't be a one-off. It's something that is growing in terms of interest and motivation from that set of stakeholders."

Boards should encourage a conversation between the company's tax specialists and its sustainability experts so that each group is aware of the other's priorities and can take them into account in its own work. Next should be nudging management to be more transparent in its approach to tax issues. All too often, such disclosures take place far too late, likely either as a tactic to fend off a crisis or because they are required by regulators, as is the case in some extractive industries. "You really don't want to be in either of these positions," d'Adhemar says. "Voluntary reporting provides an opportunity to look inside the business and see if this is a material topic for you." Birgit Noergaard, who sits on the boards of several multinational companies, suggests that boards should make a point of comparing a country's nominal tax rates with the actual taxes that the company pays "and make sure that you can explain the difference." Companies also need to be aware that tax savings can be offset by uncounted extra costs in the way business is conducted. According to Noergaard, a good test of whether a company is acting responsibly is to answer a simple question: Can you defend your tax structure to a tabloid journalist?

The Pay Gap

Even before COVID-19, boards were coming to appreciate the importance of executive pay as a driver of change within a company. The pandemic has undoubtedly reinforced that trend, with more and more companies tying bonuses and other remuneration to environmental, social, and governance criteria. Ganu cites the example of a client that tied its chief executive's 2020 bonus to the rate of spread of COVID-19 in the company relative to the general population, as part of a drive to improve employees' health and safety:

> One could argue that the management team should have done all these things anyway, because they were the right thing to do. But sometimes rewarding management for going above and beyond what is expected becomes really important, particularly during transformations or times of crises such as a COVID year, when you have cash flow and financial liability concerns. A lot of management teams have asked the question: "Could we defer certain programs? Could we cut certain costs? Let's look at this ESG stuff next year." But the more progressive boards have held the line and stood fast, stating that this is not about trade-offs. This is about doing both. It's very much an "and" not an "either-or" proposition.

Most recently, the pandemic has shone a brighter—and mostly unflattering—light on the yawning gap between the pay of senior executives and other employees. According to the Economic Policy Institute, executive compensation has ballooned more than tenfold (940 percent) since 1978, while the average employee's wages have crept up only 12 percent.[87] This gap is now widely viewed as a key contributor to widening income inequality, a trend exacerbated by the pandemic. Not surprisingly, it is attracting widespread attention from anti-poverty activists, the media, politicians, and even shareholders. Among boards, the realization is taking hold that a glaring imbalance in pay can hurt employee morale, weaken customer loyalty, and encourage "say on pay" resolutions from shareholders at annual meetings.

The experience of video-game maker Electronic Arts is a cautionary tale. The California-based company was forced to overhaul its executive compensation and bonus scheme in 2021 after shareholders rejected its 2020 plan due mainly to a special round of stock awards that resulted in the chief executive being paid 56 percent more than the median for CEOs in peer companies. Several proxy advisers, whose recommendations are often decisive in determining the votes of institutional shareholders, expressed concerns about this huge disparity. One of them, Institutional Shareholder Services (ISS), warned that such a gap would have "a ratcheting effect on executive compensation." Under the revised plan, Electronic Arts agreed not to grant any special equity awards in 2021, and some executives even ended up with a smaller compensation package.[88]

One way of avoiding such a backlash is transparency. Boards need to set and, if necessary, lower expectations early on, especially among senior executives. They must also ensure that they can clearly and convincingly explain how they set executive compensation, including bonuses. If the CEO is doing a good job, he/she/they should obviously be well compensated. But if the opposite is true, the board should ensure that the CEO and other members of the management team are seen to be sharing the pain. Setting these parameters often involves complex judgments based as much on instinct as on hard numbers. Most important is to gauge the likely reaction from all relevant constituencies, and to ensure that the company's reputation remains unsullied.

Competent boards should also insist that incentives are aligned with the long-term goals of the company, which means using relevant yardsticks to measure performance. All too often, boards make the mistake of settling either on inappropriate measurements or on criteria that are out of date and no longer fit the company's future direction. They should take care that incentives encourage executives to take neither too much nor too little risk, and that they dovetail with the culture of the organization. For example, a start-up may have a very different tolerance for risk than a stable, well-established company.

The bottom line is that a misguided compensation policy can cause huge headaches, from unwanted media attention to a proxy battle. Mark Reid, global leader of Willis Towers Watson's rewards business, also singles out the potentially corrosive effect of disagreements over pay on the relationship between management and board members. Such disputes, he notes, can break down long-standing goodwill and erode trust. As a result, "the board ends up spending way more time than is appropriate to sort out executive pay issues. The relationship can become quite dysfunctional, and the business really gets personal. That's often not a mistake of design or structure, but of communication between the different parties."

Investing for a Sustainable Future

Every shareholder wants to invest in a company that will succeed in the long term rather than in one at risk of disappearing. But identifying the likely winners has become more challenging in recent years given fast-moving shifts in consumer preferences, technology, and global geopolitical developments, including climate change. One consequence of these forces is that the long-term value of once-prized assets will be impaired by disruptive events such as rising sea levels, the move away from fossil fuels, and extreme weather.

Impaired—also known as stranded—assets could have a serious impact in coming years on corporate balance sheets in a wide swathe of industries. Beyond considering the usual financial measures such as payback scenarios, discounted cash flow, and depreciation rates, boards should thus be pressing management for information that offers clues to possible future impairment. Some of the questions worth asking: Will new products have a lower carbon footprint than existing ones? Will those new products be recyclable? Will a new plant or building have a lower carbon footprint? Will it be able to meet future standards for energy-efficient buildings? Is the new structure in an area vulnerable to flooding or other extreme weather? And so on.

The point of these questions is that investment decisions taken today will have an impact on the business not only next year and the year after but as far ahead as 2050 and perhaps even beyond. Every board needs to be thinking about what the world will look like in twenty or thirty years' time and planning investments accordingly. Board members may not need to know the value assigned to every asset, but they should have confidence that management has given sufficient thought to long-term asset values. That process may include asking what advice management has based its decisions on, and whether that advice has taken account of the changing world around us, and the risks it has created. Simply signing off on the accounts because "that's how we did it last year" is no longer an option for a competent board.

A good primer for this work is the *Essential Guide to Capex: A Practical Guide to Embedding Sustainability into Capital Investment Appraisal*, published by the A4S CFO Leadership Network, an offshoot of The Prince's Accounting for Sustainability Project.[89] The guide spells out how businesses can adapt their investment appraisal processes in a pragmatic and systematic way to integrate social and environmental issues. It also demonstrates how including sustainability in this process can reduce finance costs, improve access to capital, and open up new revenue opportunities. One small example: a green retrofit could enhance the resale value of a building.

Boards should also bear in mind the cost of inaction. Timely measures to mitigate sustainability risks are typically far less costly than trying to adapt later in the midst of a crisis. The board and the chief financial officer, in particular, have crucial roles to play in setting the right tone for this work by helping key decision-makers within the company understand the link between sustainability and improved investment performance.

CASE STUDY: PATAGONIA

Patagonia has long enjoyed a reputation as one of the world's most socially responsible businesses. Since 1985, long before pollution and climate change captured public attention, the California-based outdoor clothing maker pledged to earmark 1 percent of its sales to preserve and restore the natural environment. By 2020, it had given more than US$140 million in cash and in-kind donations to grassroots environmental groups seeking to make a difference in their communities.

Patagonia has also broken with traditional corporate attitudes towards taxation and pay. When it shuttered its thirty-nine North American stores and suspended its online business in May 2020 as the COVID-19 pandemic took hold, it vowed to continue paying employees their expected wages. It took an especially bold step after Congress approved US$1.5 trillion in tax cuts in 2017, including a substantial drop in corporate tax rates. Privately held Patagonia announced that it would donate its own tax savings to environmental groups. "We are putting US$10 million back into the planet because our home needs it more than we do," the company's then-CEO Rose Marcario declared in a letter. "Taxes protect the most vulnerable in our society, our public lands, and other life-giving resources ... In spite of this, the Trump administration initiated a corporate tax cut, threatening these services at the expense of our planet."[90]

Patagonia has led the way in other areas, too. In 2016, it decided to withdraw from the annual outdoor retailer trade show in Salt Lake City in protest against moves by then-Utah governor Gary Herbert to rescind a federal decree proclaiming the 200,000-acre Bears Ears area as a national monument. Numerous other companies joined the boycott, forcing the Outdoor Retailer and the Outdoor Industry Association to seek an alternative site for the show in a state with more friendly public land policies.

■■■

Guidelines for Competent Boards

» Be aware that more and more stakeholders view tax optimization, no matter how legal, as unethical and irresponsible.

» Stay abreast of changing tax policies and codes of conduct around the world that encourage ESG investments.

» Regularly question and assess the long-term value of the company's assets.

» Devise effective long-term investment strategies to avoid risks associated with impairment losses and stranded assets.

» Question the socio-economic and reputational impact of financial decisions. What is the impact on the environment? How will workers, customers, and society be affected? Do you risk harming the environment or stakeholders in ways that could easily be avoided and turned towards a positive impact?

» Consider emerging focus areas of compensation policy, such as internal pay equity, compensation incentives below the executive suite, and wider use of non-financial measures for compensation plans.

» Consider greater transparency in setting compensation, and measures to justify merit-based compensation.

» Expect intensified scrutiny of compensation practices if your company has benefited from public support, including during the pandemic.

Ten Key Questions

(Recommended exercise: Ask each director to answer these questions independently. Then compare and discuss. More details on page 231.)

1. Has your board discussed an approach to paying tax that goes beyond purely legal commitments?
2. Which board members have the expertise to exercise oversight on tax issues?
3. Has the company considered the impact of the 15 percent global minimum corporate tax?
4. Has the board discussed the impact of tax planning and CEO pay on the company's reputation?
5. Have you encouraged an exchange of ideas between your company's tax experts and the sustainability team?

6. How often does the board review and amend the company's investment strategy?
7. Has the board considered the opportunities associated with an investment strategy focused on outside stakeholders and communities?
8. Is your company investing enough in digital interfaces with customers and suppliers?
9. Are you aware of the pay gap between the CEO and the average employee, and between gender identity, race, ethnicity, age, etc.? Do you know how you compare to your peers?
10. Is executive pay tied to value creation, including ESG measures and wider measures of socio-economic well-being?

REFLECTIONS

"An alignment between the company's performance and the CEO's pay is becoming more paramount. It is almost incomprehensible to shareholders when the CEO's pay goes up while the shareholders' value goes down due to poor performance."

–Daniel Oh, managing director, corporate governance, Morrow Sodali

"The idea that you pay no tax and do not contribute to the society that makes your corporate building possible is, I think, not acceptable to most people."

–*Catherine McCall, executive director, Canadian Coalition for Good Governance*

"When you're not transparent, then you give the impression that you have something to hide, and hiding has to do with shame."

–*Victor van Kommer, director of tax services and member of the executive board, International Bureau of Fiscal Documentation*

CHAPTER 10

What Stakeholders Want ...
But Are Not Getting

"Stakeholder concerns are shareholder concerns. The
increasing focus by investors, consumers, and other
stakeholders on sustainability is directly influencing
value creation."

*–Jane Diplock, chair, Abu Dhabi Global Market Regulatory
Committee; director, Value Reporting Foundation*

WHY THIS MATTERS

A yawning gap has opened in recent years between investors' view of a company's transparency and communication,
and the company's own opinion. While boards and management press resolutely ahead with their traditional quarterly
earnings calls, financial presentations, and annual reports,
regulators and shareholders are demanding greater disclosure of "not-yet-financial" risks and performance indicators,
such as diversity, climate change, cybersecurity, supply
chain, and labour practices. Activism is growing on all these
fronts, especially among young people, and companies dare
not ignore it. Recent proxy seasons have seen rising investor
support for shareholder proposals related to environmental,
social, and governance issues. Bonnie Saynay, global head

of ESG research and data strategy at ISS ESG, a division of Institutional Shareholder Services (ISS), estimates that these topics were raised 205 times during investor calls in the fourth quarter of 2020. Kingsdale Advisors's Wes Hall adds that "people want to know that you have a social conscience as a company."

Yet most boards are still in the early stages of figuring out how to provide this information. Some have little idea of the factors most material to their companies' long-term growth, yet that is precisely what investors are interested in, especially those—such as pension funds—with commitments stretching decades into the future.

Engagement with shareholders and other stakeholders was once viewed as an optional, precautionary effort designed to disclose whatever management chose to disclose (which was usually as little as possible) and to garner support for new corporate initiatives. But engagement is fast becoming an essential attribute of forward-looking board members and executives. The convergence of political, social, and financial risks is forcing boards to rethink their approach. Waiting for the annual proxy season to discover that shareholders may not support a company's decisions can spell disaster. If boards are to deliver the best possible results to stakeholders, including shareholders, they need to be aware of those stakeholders' views, and that can only happen if they are actively engaged. A company lacking stakeholder engagement risks undermining its reputation and attracting shareholder activism.

The pandemic has added fresh urgency to the need for engagement and transparency. Issues such as employee health and safety, supply-chain stability, executive pay, and remote working have been very much on shareholders' minds over the past two years, resulting in a slew of shareholder resolutions on these topics during the 2021 proxy season. Beyond pandemic-related issues, investors are asking for more information on diversity, equity and inclusion efforts, labour practices, and policies on political campaign contributions and lobbying activities. A sign of the direction the wind is blowing comes from Patrick McGurn, ISS's former head of strategic research and analysis, who warns that "starting in 2022, if boards have not responded by bringing some additional diversity into their boardrooms, they can expect to see that advisers are going to consider at least recommending against heads of nominating committees or other board positions in order to really light a fire under them to be responsive to shareholder concerns in this area."

How to Prepare

While financial reporting has been standardized and digitized for many years, that is not yet the case for sustainability reporting and ESG disclosures. That raises numerous challenges for boards, among them: deciding what outside forces are material to the business, what standards to apply in presenting ESG information, and just how far a director's fiduciary duty extends to disclose this information.

As discussed in earlier chapters, this uncertainty has already triggered a confusing—and sometimes competing—array of standards and frameworks produced by an alphabet soup of non-governmental organizations. The good news is that these groups have begun to realize that collaboration and consolidation are essential if their work is to have a meaningful impact on corporate disclosure. It may be a while before the dust settles, but in the meantime, competent boards would be well advised to familiarize themselves with at least some of the reporting initiatives highlighted in chapter 2, in particular the Task Force on Climate-related Financial Disclosures (TCFD) and the Prototype Climate-Related Financial Disclosure Standard. The prototype is emerging as an influential template for future reporting standards and the TCFD is already embedded into regulation in many countries.

For an example of the value of non-financial performance indicators, boards may also wish to review the return on sustainability investment (ROSI) designed by the NYU Stern Center for Sustainable Business in collaboration with the pharmaceutical, automotive, retail, apparel, and food industries, among others. Tensie Whelan, the centre's director, describes the initiative in more detail:

> To help identify the implementation of certain sustainability strategies, we have identified nine practices that drive value in a variety of different ways. These include: innovation and growth, operational efficiency, employee engagement, productivity, retention, reduction of risk, and supplier and customer loyalty.
>
> We found that one company's waste reduction strategies resulted in $235 million in extra pre-tax income. They didn't know that because the sustainability strategy, the benefits, and the practices were in a variety of different places, and nobody had set things up to track the financial returns from the beginning. They just saw it as a cost of compliance not as an area for value creation.

In the apparel sector, we have worked with Eileen Fisher to monetize their circularity strategy. They give their customers a coupon to return gently used Eileen Fisher clothes. They take anything that's not wearable and upcycle it into felts for bags and pillows and things like that. Anything that is reusable, they clean and mend and include in their Renew line. The financial benefits are several. Obviously, one is the very low margin for this product. Secondly, when people come to buy that product, they buy more—so there are incremental sales. Also, the coupon brought in people to buy more. They had significant earned media, which we valued for them as well. But the most interesting was that the Renew line brought in a new demographic of younger customers. They had no acquisition costs associated with bringing in a demographic that they had struggled to reach in prior years. A traditional analysis would have asked, "How much should we make on selling this product line?" without taking account of all these other benefits that accrue.

Engagement and collaboration also require a different mindset from the past. Instead of going it alone and seeing every encounter in terms of winners and losers, the emphasis should be on negotiation and trust. Overcoming deep-rooted environmental and societal problems is best done in partnership with suppliers, employees, and even NGOs and governments. If nothing else, every board needs to prepare for the day when it finds itself in the crosshairs of an activist shareholder or being blindsided by a blistering social media campaign. The chances of successfully defending itself—or even avoiding such a situation entirely—are greatly enhanced if board members can showcase their expertise, build self-awareness, expand their understanding of what shareholders and stakeholders expect, and, in the process, build loyalty and trust.

Building Trust

Many boards don't know their investors well enough, thereby leaving the door wide open for an assault by activists and other disgruntled shareholders. Often, a road show or a quarterly earnings call is spent telling investors what management wants them to hear, instead of listening to their suggestions and concerns. Boards and managements also typically spend too little time explaining the rationale for key decisions. Instead, they—sometimes stubbornly—cling to underperforming assets or businesses, digging in against critics until it's too late. What investors are looking for is honesty and openness rather than a scripted sales pitch. By being more proactive and transparent, companies can build trust, ensuring that shareholders remain loyal if and when the activists come knocking. Bjarne Graven Larsen, chair of Nordic Investment Opportunities, adds that "sometimes I even prefer somebody who says the politically incorrect things because they are frustrated about something. Then you can actually have a discussion." However, board members and managers should always remember to keep the tone authentic.

Building trust involves several steps, not all of them easy. A company should make sure that it knows not only who its shareholders are but also how they make their voting decisions—whether through a governance team, a proxy committee, or on the recommendation of a proxy adviser.

Management and board members then need to give careful thought to the most effective ways of engaging with the investors who are most important to the company. To avoid unpleasant surprises, the board should insist on regular feedback from meetings with these investors. Kingsdale Advisors encourages clients to move beyond the traditional quarterly earnings presentation where executives talk about the performance of the business, and instead organize what Wes Hall calls a "governance road show" led by independent board members. This format encourages a more candid exchange of views, including, for example, about the CEO's performance.

Investors are also looking for more information and data. Those disclosures are more than just the hard numbers and should provide insights into the company's priorities and values. Furthermore, the emphasis should be on the future rather than on the past or present. Under the latest guidance from the US Securities and Exchange Commission, companies must disclose their forward-looking strategy. A competent board will do this within a set timeframe, connecting it to the company's plans for long-term capital allocation, sustainability, and executive compensation. The messaging should be concise, simple, and as specific as possible.

CDP's Paul Dickinson suggests that boards deal with their investors as they would with a health insurer:

> Let's say that the patient, or the insured party, fills out a questionnaire and explains how they're living: what they weigh, how much exercise they take, if they smoke, if they drink. Now, imagine you're the insurer, and the patient doesn't even bother to fill out that information. Are you going to put a risk premium on them? Of course, you are.

After fifteen years of providing this service, I can say that we've got essentially the right system operating at the right scale. I think the 9,600 corporations that report through us to over 800 investors have validated this system.

New Partnerships

As part of the drive to broaden their horizons, boards should encourage management to tackle sustainability issues in partnership with other businesses, relevant government agencies, NGOs, and even activist groups. Herbert Heitmann notes that "NGOs are too often seen as the enemies. They are not. They are just another legitimate group of stakeholders. Pick the right ones, and you can find great partners to advance your business. If you pick the wrong ones, you expose yourself to even more trouble and you waste resources." Education and listening should be key parts of the process. In other words, a competent board will go out of its way to meet with these groups and hear what they have to say about the company's business practices and culture.

Many such collaborative initiatives are already underway—for example, moves to improve labour conditions in the South Asian apparel industry and a drive to extract palm oil in a more environmentally friendly way.[91,92]

Rules of Engagement

Listening to stakeholders' concerns and then perhaps changing tack can be a time-consuming and at times frustrating process for a company. Nonetheless, those that make the effort to reach out in this way have a distinct advantage over those that don't.

The reason is that more and more investors have come to realize that engagement with boards and management often leads to a more fruitful outcome than divestment. Pulling out becomes an option only if the company is unresponsive or shows no willingness to rectify its malpractices. What's more, notes Federated Hermes's Timothy Youmans, "there's a difference between active shareholding and activism. Talking to investors is the number one way for boards to inoculate themselves against activism and proxy fights."

A fine example of active shareholding is Climate Action 100+, an investor-led initiative that is pressing the world's largest corporate greenhouse gas emitters to take action on climate change. The group has brought together several existing initiatives in different parts of the world. Every member pledges to seek three main commitments from at least one of 167 companies identified as major emitters:

- Implement a strong governance framework on climate change

- Take action to reduce greenhouse gas emissions across the value chain

- Provide enhanced corporate disclosure

Even so, Nancy Lockhart, a George Weston director, takes the view that boards need to pick their battles:

> It's not a company's job to answer every little stakeholder group. What's really important is that the company be aware of the issues that are raised, accept or reject them based on science or data, and deal with the ones that are most important. You can't do everything. So you've got to

pick the ones that have the biggest impact. And let's not forget that there are all kinds of interest groups that have their own agendas that don't necessarily relate to anything other than their own agendas. You've got to weed those out.

Materiality

As alluded to in chapter 2, the concept of materiality has come to be accepted as a key building block in determining how a company should engage with its stakeholders. At its most basic, it refers simply to the issues that matter to investors. Importantly, however, materiality no longer covers only risks and opportunities that have a direct impact on the profit and loss statement or the balance sheet. Regulators and investors are steadily broadening the definition to include any external development that may have an impact on the company's future well-being or sustainability.

The concept has also been expanded in recent years to what is known as "double materiality," which refers not only to the forces creating value and risk for a company but also those that the company itself has a hand in creating and that could have an impact on society. Carbon emissions and income inequality are two prime examples. One of the key decisions in the drive to create widely accepted sustainability standards is whether reporting should include double as well as single materiality.

So, how does a board determine materiality? For now, there is no clear answer to the question. Every company is likely to look at an issue through a different lens, using a different test. But there are undoubtedly some common threads. As Allen

White, co-founder and former CEO of the Global Reporting Initiative, puts it:

> If you hear from ten thousand customers that there's something amiss with a product or service, then you have a problem. You have a problem of reputation and quality. You should not deny it and you need to report on it, because when stakeholders see disclosures of that nature, it builds trust. And pre-emptive, anticipatory disclosure is vastly superior to a newspaper journalist knocking on your door and saying, "I just heard that ten people are in the hospital due to a drug or food product gone bad." So conducting continuous monitoring and research of customer views is critical to long-term competitiveness. Boards have a vested interest—indeed, an obligation—to get this right. Fiduciary duty requires nothing less.

Tensie Whelan has some advice on how to tackle the process:

> Start with your strategy, understand the material ESG issues, and determine which issues you're going to focus on, from both an opportunity and risk perspective. Identify what your key performance indicators are for those sustainability elements and apply them just as you would with your business strategy. Then look again at the material issues, as you will have done initially. The Sustainability Accounting Standards Board, the Task Force on Climate-related Financial Disclosures, and other frameworks can help you understand how to report the material issues against a recognized standard. And then, ideally, you get a third-party auditor to point out where this isn't working well; this also gives credibility to the results. You should be going through

the same type of process with your ESG key performance indicators as you do with all your business indicators. When people ask why you are not giving them a hundred metrics, you can say: "Because this is our strategy, this is why we're focused on these metrics, and we're not going to be reporting on things that aren't material to our business strategy."

Integrated Reporting

Many companies have tended to relegate ESG issues to their own silos, viewing them as distinct parts of the organization rather than as elements that permeate almost everything the company does. In these situations, the chief financial officer and the sustainability team have operated quite separately from one another. That is quickly changing, however, as smart business leaders understand that sustainability and financial performance go hand in hand. One obvious way of recognizing that symbiotic relationship is through integrated reporting.

A number of influential investors already use integrated reporting to drive their decisions and are urging more companies to adopt the practice. Proxy advisers report a surge of interest in integrated financial and sustainability reporting since early 2020, even among investors normally slow to change their proxy voting guidelines. Increasingly, institutions are willing to support shareholder resolutions or vote against members of boards of directors if they detect inaction or a lack of attention to issues such as climate and diversity. We can thus expect to see more ESG material included in mainstream financial disclosures, such as the annual report, rather than in a separate sustainability report. Competent boards will keep pushing for sustainability to be integrated to the maximum degree possible with every other corporate function.

Richard Howitt, former CEO of the International Integrated Reporting Council, cautions that this is a learning process and that "if companies wait until they can do a perfect integrated report, they'll wait forever." Instead, he recommends a gradual approach stretching over at least four years, as follows:

> Perhaps in year one, they commit to integrated reporting and using the principles of the international integrated reporting framework. By year two, they might well have an analysis of the resources and relationships the company draws upon to undertake its business. By year three, they might have translated that into a stronger, clearer definition of their own business model. And by year four, they might have fully integrated key financial and non-financial performance indicators in the long term as well as the short term. Companies will do it in different ways, and it's a learning process. But if board members decide they want to adopt this approach, all they have to do is blow the whistle to get started.

CASE STUDY: ØRSTED

One company that has successfully managed the transition from passive to active engagement is Ørsted, Denmark's largest energy utility. Ørsted has undergone a dramatic transformation since its inception in 1972 as Dansk Naturgas, and later as Dansk Olie og

Naturgas. For the first thirty years of its existence, its business centred on coal-fired power plants in Denmark, and offshore oil and gas drilling rigs in various other parts of Europe. In 2006, however, it decided to shift its focus to green energy, closing its coal-fired plants and putting its resources instead into offshore wind farms. As of 2020, the Danish company was the world's leader in offshore wind power, with a 30 percent market share; it forecast that it would produce enough power for more than 30 million people by 2025.[93]

Stakeholder engagement has been a key pillar of the transition strategy. In 2007, for example, the company began fostering a dialogue with activist groups such as Greenpeace, the World Wildlife Fund and the Danish Society for Nature Conservation. Rob Morris, a senior editor at the London Business School, noted in an article that Ørsted "had to convince people that the future business could be as successful as the old one."[94] One example was a lengthy op-ed piece in Denmark's *Politiken* newspaper written by then-CEO Anders Eldrup in which he stressed that transformation would not be an overnight miracle. Eldrup publicly debated the company's climate action strategy with Greenpeace's then-executive director Mads Flarup Christensen at a 2009 meeting hosted by the Copenhagen Business School.

While the Danish government still owns 50.1 percent of Ørsted's shares, the company has been listed on the Copenhagen stock exchange since 2016.[95] The following year, it opened another useful avenue to tell its story to international investors by launching its first green bond.

"A lot of it starts with a company needing to be clear about what its purpose and its real priorities are, and that can be quite difficult to formulate," says Ørsted's current board chair Thomas Thune Andersen. "We have a wide debate about strategy that covers everything from the annual strategy plan to the long-term strategy, to our strategic priorities. If you're able to really explain what your strategic priorities are, you're able to get the shareholders and others to buy in."

Ørsted now conducts a thorough materiality assessment each year, which involves identifying its most material stakeholders as well as assessing shareholder priorities and how these priorities intersect with society's overall challenges. It has identified five key stakeholder groups: political stakeholders and authorities, local communities, employees, investors and shareholders, and NGOs/multiple stakeholder networks. The company has a specific interest in each group. Political stakeholders are vital allies in its plans to develop green energy. Local communities and employees provide valuable input on skills, talent retention, education, and local environmental initiatives. Investors expect strong financial returns as well as robust performance on environmental, social, and governance issues. Finally, the company engages NGOs and multi-stakeholder networks on topics such as biomass sustainability and human rights. It has worked to strengthen implementation of the UN Guiding Principles on Business and Human Rights and has identified minerals and metals in its supply chain where environmental and human rights risks are greatest. The Danish company also has no problem collaborating with other utilities to develop wind farm projects. For example, in March 2020, it joined forces with Japan's Tokyo Electric Power Company Holdings to bid for an offshore wind power project in Chiba prefecture, near Tokyo.[96] The two companies have several other joint projects.

Ørsted has set a target of net-zero carbon emissions by 2025 and no carbon emissions at all by 2040.[97] *Corporate Knights* magazine named it the world's most sustainable energy company for three years in a row, from 2019 to 2021, and ranked it number two across all sectors in 2021. But sustainability has not come at the expense of financial performance.[98] Ørsted's market value has more than doubled since its listing in 2016, surpassing rivals such as BP with a far greater dependence on fossil fuels. It achieved a 10 percent return on capital and a 4 percent advance in operating profit in 2020. As of mid-2021, its share price had almost quadrupled since the 2016 initial public offering.

■ ■ ■

Guidelines for Competent Boards

» Know who your shareholders are and how they make voting decisions.

» Be sure that directors engage with shareholders as well as other stakeholders before and beyond proxy season.

» Draw up a concise "statement of purpose" unique to your company that spells out who your key stakeholders are and what issues are material to them. It should also detail long-term financial and ESG goals.

» Examine which sustainability risks and opportunities are material to your company's business, and how they might fit into one or more of the emerging reporting standards.

» Seek out partnerships with suppliers, customers, competitors, governments, NGOs, and relevant academics to tackle the risks facing your company.

» Aim to publish an integrated report.

» Ensure that you are proactively engaged in and sign off on sustainability, ESG, or integrated reports.

» Prepare for further integration of financial and non-financial filings by staying abreast of reporting developments (see chapter 2).

» Be sure that internal governance mechanisms match your professed policies.

» Consider expanding proxy disclosures beyond legal requirements.

Ten Key Questions

(Recommended exercise: Ask each director to answer these questions independently. Then compare and discuss. More details on page 231.)

1. Do you have the right board structure to address and communicate the specific risks that threaten your industry and your company?

2. What progress is your company making towards compiling an integrated report?

3. Which board members have the expertise to exercise oversight in ESG reporting and identifying issues material to the company's business?

4. How are material issues identified, and could this process be improved?

5. Is your company using its financial reporting to reinforce its sustainability goals?

6. Are you discussing ESG issues at investor days and on quarterly earnings calls?

7. What is the board doing to stay up to date with the evolving concerns of shareholders, employees, suppliers, customers, regulators, and other stakeholders?

8. What is the board doing to open channels of communication with ESG activist investors?

9. How is the company engaging shareholders on material ESG issues ahead of the annual proxy season? Are you open to organizing a governance roadshow?

10. What procedures are in place to ensure maximum transparency and quality in company communications, including regulatory filings?

REFLECTIONS

"If you can't tell me or an investor or the CEO what you think the purpose of the company is, then something really big is missing."

–Robert Eccles, eminent academic adviser on global ESG integration and reporting, Boston Consulting Group (BCG)

"The good corporation is an integral part of the network it operates in. It has a relationship with its clients, suppliers, neighbours. It does not live in a vacuum. All of these are not on the balance sheet, but if you are aware of them and you manage them, you clearly have an edge."

–Hakan Lucius, head of corporate responsibility and civil society, European Investment Bank

CHAPTER 11

Stewards of the Future

"Stewardship is the accountability one has for leaving the company—with all its stakeholders—stronger than when you arrived. How can you best help the company navigate the path to its best future?"

–Eric Wetlaufer, director, TMX Group and Investment Management Corporation of Ontario (IMCO)

WHY THIS MATTERS

The insights shared in this book have one common message: the companies with the best chance of thriving in years to come will be guided by leaders with the foresight and determination to tackle the daunting challenges that confront all of humankind. They will not be consumed by next quarter's or even year's financial results and share price. Rather, their gaze will be on the bigger issues shaping our society—global development, climate change, bio-diversity, cybersecurity, inequality, and so on—and how those issues will shape their businesses.

None of those leaders will be more influential in setting the course of the business than the board of directors. After all, it is the board that hires, fires, and guides the chief executive. The directors approve the company's long-term plans and oversee how the CEO and the senior management team implement them. The board is the custodian of the corporate culture, setting an example for the entire organization. It is the board that must decide whether to step on the accelerator or apply the brakes, and it is the board's responsibility to ensure that the company behaves as a good citizen wherever it operates. In short, the board must ensure that the company acts not so much as the owner of its assets—whether they be financial resources, land, water rights, data, or even its workers' time—but rather as a good steward.

So what does a corporate steward of the future look like? As I suggest in the introduction to this book, a good yardstick is the Seventh Generation Principle followed by the Indigenous Haudenosaunee Confederacy in northeast North America. The Haudenosaunee believe that the decisions we make today should keep the world in a sustainable state seven generations from now. Corporate directors can follow this precept by asking themselves some simple questions when weighing a course of action that will determine the business's future: What will my children and grandchildren say? What will our customers and suppliers say? What will our employees say? Laura Storm, co-author of *Regenerative Leadership*, offers another perspective. She recommends thinking of a company as a forest. The trees need sunlight and water to grow and provide shelter and sustenance for the animals and plants that surround them. As anyone who has walked through a lush forest knows, it lifts the spirits and inspires respect. In much the same way, good corporate stewards will be sustained and nourished by those around them, while also contributing to society's well-being.

One outstanding example of this model is Interface, the Atlanta-based maker of floor coverings founded by Ray Anderson, who managed to combine the roles of captain of industry and steward of the future.[99] "I had a revelation about what industry is doing to our planet," Anderson told an audience in London in 1999. "I stood convicted as a plunderer of the earth. In the future, people like me will go to jail." He announced at the same event that Interface was "changing course to become sustainable—to grow without damaging the earth and manufacture without pollution, waste, or fossil fuels." Anderson vowed that Interface, a heavy petrochemicals consumer, would shrink its carbon footprint and other environmental costs to zero by 2020. Anderson died in 2011, but his company was able to proclaim eight years later that it had met his target a year ahead of schedule. "What started out as the right thing to do quickly became the smart thing," Anderson told a business conference in 2005. I had the privilege of meeting Ray Anderson once in New York, and he left as big an impression on me as on likely everyone else he spoke to.

As Anderson and Interface have shown, corporate stewardship is about instilling the right values—or, to put it another way, adopting the right moral compass to sustain the natural, social, human, and, yes, financial capital that the business has been blessed with. The company must meet the "sunrise, sunshine, and sunset" test. Sunrise refers to its willingness and ability to seize new opportunities as they arise. It passes the sunshine part of the test if it can appear on the front page of tomorrow's newspaper without feeling shame or embarrassment. It will make it past sunset if it can, in a responsible manner, shut down activities that have outlived their usefulness and can no longer be considered sustainable. Figure 11.1, compiled by the International Integrated Reporting Council, illustrates how those values are created, preserved, or eroded over time.

FIGURE 11.1

Process through which value is created, preserved, or eroded.

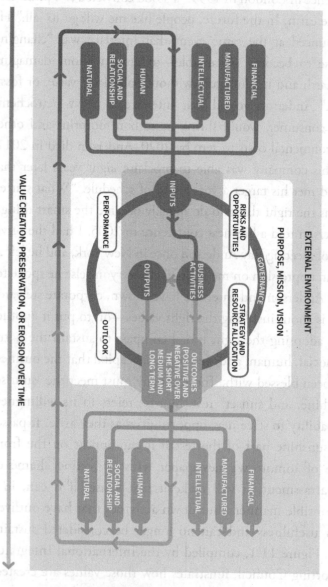

Source: International Integrated Reporting Council.

The need for wise stewards of the future was all too evident as I put the finishing touches to this book in the summer of 2021. While the global economy appeared to be returning to a semblance of its former self in the wake of the COVID-19 pandemic, the same could not be said of corporate boardrooms. Companies and their directors were under mounting pressure to adapt to the heightened urgency surrounding the earth's environmental, social, and humanitarian problems. The calls for change were coming from multiple directions, and from all parts of the world. The latest UN Climate Change Conference, scheduled for November 2021 in Glasgow, Scotland, was set to push reduction of carbon emissions even higher up corporate agendas. New initiatives were unfolding to crack down on bribery and corruption while the US Securities and Exchange Commission was girding for a more activist role in clamping down harder on questionable corporate behaviour. The International Organization for Standardization (ISO) was about to launch its guidance for governance, known as ISO 37000. A little-known hedge fund had rattled boards around the world by managing to unseat three directors of ExxonMobil, one of the world's largest energy producers. On the other side of the world, Hong Kong's Securities and Futures Commission published guidelines on ESG disclosures in June 2021 that apply to a wide range of companies, unit trusts, and mutual funds, and Singapore Exchange proposed a road map for climate-related disclosures to be made mandatory in issuers' sustainability reports and sustainability training for all directors.

Even many smaller economies were nudging their companies towards a more sustainable and socially responsible future. Take Malaysia, where a new corporate governance code, issued in April 2021, asks every board to address gaps in its ESG professional development needs. Boards should also consider whether changes in their composition or skills matrix are needed to strengthen oversight of sustainability issues.[100]

Taken together, these developments are forcing boards to confront issues and interest groups that have enjoyed little of their attention in the past. The realization is sinking in that attitudes and practices that were the norm for decades are now in the throes of far-reaching change. Companies, big and small, have little choice but to think beyond next quarter's or even next year's profit outlook, and to broaden their social and cultural boundaries. The mood is summed up by a recent Edelman survey that found that 86 percent of 33,000+ respondents expect corporate chieftains to speak publicly to the broad challenges facing society, and more than two-thirds would like them to step in when government fails to fix these issues.[101]

The reasons for this transformation are not hard to find. Modern technology enables a company's stakeholders—shareholders, customers, suppliers, activists, communities, and employees—to be more connected than ever. Those who feel disgruntled can use their smartphones to ruin a company's reputation in minutes. Yet many people feel left out, or are struggling with cyberbullying, fake news, a constant bombardment of new information, and expectations that put a strain on mental health. Elsewhere, human rights are under threat as modern slavery and economic exploitation of human life, as well as of nature, are on the rise. Some experts have compared the challenges facing corporate leaders to a tsunami—they must learn to surf or they and the companies they serve will sink.

The disparate forces buffeting business are forcing boards to ask new questions, and think in new ways. "What is our purpose? Why do we exist? How will we sustain this business over the next fifty to one hundred years successfully and profitably for all of our stakeholders?" asks Kathleen Taylor, who chairs Royal Bank of Canada's board. She adds that "those are very essential conversations for boards."

Beyond those existential questions, competent boards need to ensure that their company's values and culture reflect its purpose and the reason for its existence. They need to take a longer-term view than next quarter's financial results and share price. That means casting the net more widely in identifying the risks faced by the business, and determining which ones are most material to its future. But boards also need to appreciate the potential for new opportunities as the world changes around them. This is not a marketing exercise. If done with integrity, it will capture the hearts and minds of stakeholders, and create a lasting legacy. Ultimately, it is not about how a company spends its money; it is about how it makes its money that will determine if it is a financially sustainable business. Nothing less is required than a fresh mindset into what business's responsibilities are in the modern world, and then the determination and leadership to carry out those responsibilities.

THE BOARD OF THE FUTURE

Competent Boards recently published an overview of the competencies and qualities that will be essential for boards of directors if they are to successfully navigate the fast-moving corporate governance landscape and deliver both short-term results and long-term value creation.[102] The report asks four questions:

- What does stewardship in the twenty-first century look like?

- What does a future-prepared board member look like?

- What competencies should be demanded of board members?

- What personal traits, qualities, and perspectives are needed in the modern boardroom?

The responses suggest that effective board leadership starts with a sense of purpose informed by knowledge of the environmental, social, and governance challenges faced by the company. As Paul Druckman, chair of the World Benchmarking Alliance, puts it:

> The modern board needs to revitalize itself because wider issues than those within the company and within the capital markets are not clearly understood by many senior board members. Most boards contain members who feel they bring an independent view. But that independence has been independent of the company, not representing wider society. I don't think many of us have the skills and experience to do that.

Our survey concluded that competent boards of the future will be highly focused on co-operative decision-making and inclusiveness. They will have a driving passion to tackle systemic inequalities by expanding board diversity and promoting a more equitable decision-making process. They will apply their wisdom to make sense of information, balance the needs of all stakeholders, and then adapt their business strategy accordingly. They will have to understand how ESG issues relate to business strategy. They will have to possess not only the usual, time-tested skills and experience expected of a wise board but also a wider vision that takes account of the myriad issues—from climate change, cyber threats, and corruption to human-trafficking and ethical tax policies—that will shape the business world of tomorrow.

Stakeholders expect boards to become more diverse in the years ahead. They will have stronger representation from women, racial minorities, people with disabilities, and young people. A UBS investor survey published in June 2021 underscored the key role that younger generations are playing in shaping the boardroom of the future.[103] Almost 80 percent of investors under fifty said COVID has encouraged them to make a bigger difference in the world, compared with just half of the over-fifties respondents. Competent boards should be asking which of these age groups they spend more time with and, indeed, to what extent the under-fifties are represented on the board itself. After all, the future belongs to the young, whether boomers like it or not.

With a sharper focus on stakeholder capitalism, ESG, and systemic racial injustice, corporate actions will have to reflect the interests of all stakeholders. They will also have to be transparent enough to be noticed by those they affect. The board will have to nurture the trust and confidence of those who come into contact with the company if it hopes to drive sustainable value creation. But that can be achieved only through a collaborative process involving customers, employees, and the wider community. What's more, the board will need to accomplish all this without taking its eye off short-term financial performance. R. Gopalakrishnan, a former director of India's Tata Group, compares the challenge facing the board to the relationship between a mother and her child:

> The purpose of good corporate governance is to see how your company can be a good corporate citizen for all stake-holders, and yet make a profit. I don't see that as being very different from a mother raising a child who probably does everything for her child to be a good, responsible citizen of society. And she hopes the child also wins the Nobel Prize or becomes a professor, or whatever. It's exactly the same with corporate governance.

Agnes KY Tai, director, Great Glory Investment Corporation, points to the importance of open-mindedness.

> The world is changing so very, very fast. So having an open mind, being able to communicate, being articulate, and being able to disagree in a pleasant way are really important so that we, as a whole board, will still collec-tively be able to make informed decisions to move the company forward.

More generally, corporate stewardship in the twenty-first century will demand a high degree of accountability, com-bined with the highest standards of ethics and integrity. As the authors of an article in the Harvard Law School's *Forum on Corporate Governance* put it in mid-2020, the purpose of the corporation is to "achieve and conduct a lawful, eth-ical, profitable and sustainable business to create value over the long term."[104] ISS ESG's Bonnie Saynay asserts that "corporate stewardship is inextricably linked to responsible capitalism, which, by design, supports ongoing institutional engagement that is transparent, collaborative, and developmental in building resilient corporate cultures that ultimately impact a broader stakeholder base."

THE DIRECTOR OF THE FUTURE

What attributes will competent boards and nominating committees be looking for in board members in the years ahead? Three key traits emerged from our survey: **courage, empathy**, and **persuasiveness**.[105] Beyond that, we can expect the most sought-after directors to possess the following:

- **Curiosity** to support a culture of continuous learning and a willingness to adapt to new strategies and ever-changing expectations both within the company and among outside stakeholders. A curious mindset will also encourage fellow-directors to identify novel solutions and pursue them.

- **Inclusiveness** in terms of perspectives and lived experiences that reflect the communities in which the organization operates. Likewise, directors should insist on bringing all dimensions of diversity to the table, providing viewpoints that may have been overlooked in the past.

- **A purpose-driven mindset** that can distill the company's purpose into a vision that also reflects the shared principles and values of society as a whole.

- **The ability to communicate** how board-level actions relate to the long-term interests of the company.

- **A level of respect and transparency** that encourages an open exchange of honest opinions. Competent directors welcome conflicting arguments that ultimately produce a powerful shared vision. Board members should thus be willing not only to voice their own opinions but also to engage with others who may hold different views. This interaction greatly reduces the risk of groupthink and cultural bias.

- **Forthrightness in asking questions and a willingness to question answers.** The director of the future will value diverse opinions as an opportunity to engage with new ideas and possibly challenge the status quo, even if this may not always be comfortable. According to PwC's 2020 annual corporate directors survey, more than one-third of directors find it difficult to voice a dissenting opinion, highlighting the need for an open and respectful dialogue if the board is to deliver its best collective ideas.

- **An understanding of critical ESG issues and how to address them.** Our survey results indicate that knowledge of the United Nations sustainable development goals sets a solid foundation for developing a long-term business model. Directors can use the goals as a tool to identify the most material ESG issues and how they relate to the company's overall business strategy. The board skills matrix should reflect these competencies so stakeholders can evaluate directors' level of preparedness.[106]

- **An entrepreneurial attitude** that stimulates creative problem-solving in times of uncertainty.

Nancy Lockhart, who sits on the board of food conglomerate George Weston, emphasizes the importance of directors gaining first-hand knowledge of their company's operations:

> In the old days, boards consisted of a group of people who got together, looked at statements that management had put together, and then had a drink. There didn't seem to be any desire to get out in the field. To understand the company you're representing and to do the best job for the shareholders, you've got to get out into the field. You've got to put boots on the ground. It doesn't matter what the industry is. If it's retail, you go to stores. If it's mining, you go to mines. If it's financial services, you get to know what everybody else in the sector is doing. You've got to do the homework, and you've got to get out of the boardroom.

But knowledge must go hand in hand with humility and a willingness to acknowledge what you don't know, says R. Gopalakrishnan:

> Rather than every board member knowing everything, I would like to see directors who are humble enough to say: "I don't understand this." That's the kind of board I really enjoy. The underlying point is that board members are not taught humility, and they are not known to be humble. And if in some way, the fact that they are fallible and humble can come to them, that's far more valuable than being experts in all those subjects.

Despite the many risks and threats that confront today's boards, there is also reason for optimism. Business has entered a period of awakening, where major transformations are taking place in all corners of the globe, altering the traditional context for boardroom decision-making and heightening the expectations of corporate leaders, including boards. I am confident that revamping corporate stewardship to meet the needs of the twenty-first century will help trigger a shift in attitude towards business from despair to hope.

THE PANDEMIC'S LEGACY

We may look back on COVID-19 as a milestone in resetting expectations of corporate boards. Nine out of ten wealthy investors polled in the above-mentioned UBS survey claimed that the pandemic made them more determined to align their investments with their values. At the same time, the pandemic has forced many companies to re-examine their business practices and values, and the risks they face, ranging from how they deal with suppliers to how they attract and keep talented employees, and balance the demands of work and home. It has taught that long-term resilience depends not only on what the company is doing to sharpen internal processes and operations but also on how well prepared it is to cope with external shocks not necessarily of its own making.

Chad Holliday gives an illustration of how DuPont put this approach into practice for an item of personal protective gear known as "tie-backs" following the SARS epidemic in 2003–2004:

> The tie-back was in very high demand during SARS. So we put together a consortium once SARS was pretty well

controlled to consider whether it was a one-off, or whether there was likely to be a pandemic like that again. Talking to scientists, our conclusion was that it was going to happen again. When, how, and where we didn't know. So we took the same group of companies and asked: Shouldn't we be prepared? Shouldn't we stockpile this stuff? And perhaps we could even have an agreement among us that if one company is particularly hard hit because of where they're located, they can be backed up by the other companies. We even had a proposal to have a warehouse for this material in Memphis, Tennessee, where FedEx is headquartered. So you have a lot of enthusiasm when something like that happens, but then to stick with it over a period of time is much tougher. It's not just stockpiling. It's about overall resilience. Right now is when you should be asking the questions, not once it's over.

Annette Verschuren adds:

This is a time and an opportunity to try new things, to take action on things that you thought you could only do five years down the road. I think this is going to be the most creative time in corporate and small business history. When you're faced with the crisis that we've faced, we have to think differently and operate differently. So really take advantage of it.

Author, advisor, and master-storyteller Dov Baron makes the point that a crisis such as the COVID-19 pandemic is an excellent time for an organization to discover its true purpose and to adopt a coherent, unified vision of its future:

Nobody is going to rally around your product or your service. The deeper meaning of your organization is the thing that people will rally around. It's what keeps people loyal to you—your employees, your customers, and clients. I believe that one of the great positive things of this situation is that it will be a cleansing. There are a lot of leaders who have been holding on and not letting go. They have been micromanaging; they have stayed around much longer than they needed to; and in many ways, they were restricting the growth of their company. This will be the great cleansing; it will push a lot of them out, because you can't lead using the old way of command-and-control in this kind of situation. You have to rally people—you have to bring them together. And the one way to do that is through a unified meaning.

HOW ONE CORPORATE GOVERNANCE LEADER SEES THE FUTURE

Mervyn King is one of the world's foremost authorities on corporate governance. A former judge on South Africa's Supreme Court, he chaired the King committee that investigated corporate governance in that country. He is also chair emeritus of the Value Reporting Foundation and of the Global Reporting Initiative, and a former member of the Private Sector Advisory Group to the World Bank on corporate governance.

King shared his views on future trends in board governance and practice with me. Here are some highlights:

- Research has shown that up to 30 percent of directors couldn't really understand the financials and, worse yet, 70 percent of the directors didn't even bother reading the sustainability reports. Boards have to spend more time, in my judgment, understanding these reports and being more comfortable with material matters, defined as that which is having an impact on the three critical dimensions for sustainable development in a resource-constrained world, namely, the economy, society, and the environment.

- A company could make a million dollars pre-tax. But *how* it makes those million dollars has become the critical issue today. Because it may be that making the million dollars is having such an adverse impact on the environment, it's actually destroying the value for society. So today it has become a question of the value-creating process, rather than making a profit, which was central to the Milton Friedman thesis that the main purpose of the corporation is to make a profit, without exception.

- I'm trying to encourage boards to have millennials as members because they've got a different mindset. They see things differently, certainly from my generation. They accuse my generation of creating the global environmental crunch, which they and their children and grandchildren have to face. And they're correct.

- Some items have to be on board agendas that have never been there before. Number one is stakeholder relationships. The board has to be informed at each meeting what the relationship is between the board, the company, and its major stakeholders. The board needs informed oversight, and that comes from having a report at each meeting.

The next item which has never been on board agendas is inputs and outcomes. What are the inputs into this company as to how it makes its money? What are the activities inside the company that are making its money? And what are its outputs? Not only the product, but also the waste. What's happening to that waste, and what are the outcomes when that product goes out into society? One of the great examples was when it was alleged that Coca-Cola was one of the reasons for obesity in children. That was an impact, an outcome. One of the critical outcomes is how climate change is impacting the business of the company and its supply chain. Then there's species extinction. Extinction accounting is suddenly becoming a reality.

The third item for the agenda is IT governance and cybersecurity. If you look at SEC filings, the greatest risk to businesses is climate change, and the second greatest is cybersecurity. IT governance and cybersecurity should be on your agenda.

The fourth item that board agendas have never had and should have is integrated functions. We all know the acronym GRC—governance, risk, and compliance. Which body has oversight over governance, risk, and compliance? It's the board. So you should have that integrated function. The company secretary, the chief risk officer, the internal auditor, etc.—all of them should be making sure they inform each other and know what's going on, with ultimate oversight from the board.

Finally, board agendas these days are incomplete without a discussion of supply-chain management, and the risks and opportunities that the business faces from climate change. When we have millennials on the board discussing these items, they will discuss them in a much different manner than male, pale, and stale directors.

Guidelines for Competent Boards

» Keep your eyes on the future.
» Focus on the big picture. Leave day-to-day operations to management.
» Familiarize yourself with global ESG trends.
» Make boardroom diversity a priority.
» Encourage a variety of opinions and respectful disagreement around the boardroom table.
» Add these items to every board meeting agenda: stakeholder relationships, inputs/outcomes, cybersecurity, and integrated functions.
» Examine all the company's outputs, not only the products it makes.
» Enroll in Competent Boards's certificate program. For details, go to **www.competentboards.com**.

Ten Key Questions

(Recommended exercise: Ask each director to answer these questions independently. Then compare and discuss. More details on page 231.)

1. What will be different about your company's board in 2030 compared to now?

2. As you see it, what new competencies should be added to your board in coming years?

3. Similarly, what personal traits, qualities, and perspectives are currently missing from your board?

4. What are you doing to bring fresh perspectives to your board from younger people and individuals without previous board experience?

5. What indicators would you use to determine sound corporate governance?

6. Name five companies that have strong corporate governance. What do they have in common?

7. To what extent are members of your board willing to listen to views contrary to their own?

8. Do board members spend time gaining first-hand knowledge of the company's operations and talking to employees, suppliers, customers, NGOs, and other stakeholders?

9. Has your board commissioned alternative scenario plans? If not, why not?

10. In the event of another global crisis, what should corporate leaders prioritize: Cutting costs to ensure shareholder returns? The survival of suppliers? Balancing the survival of the company with keeping employees safe and employed? Or some other focus?

REFLECTIONS

"Today's board members must not only bring their current expertise and experience to the boardroom but also recognize the importance of continuing learning and development. They must be flexible, working collaboratively with board members and executives to understand and manage the accelerating changes faced by companies, particularly from an ESG perspective."

–*Judith Mosely, non-executive director, BlackRock World Mining Trust*

"Step back a second and say: 'What really would make me feel like I was successful as a business leader and as a board member? What questions will my grandkids ask about what we're doing and what we've done? Will it be whether our earnings per share went up three or four per cent, or will it be that we did something larger and made people's lives better while doing it?'"

–*Andrew Winston, founder, Winston Eco-Strategies.*

"As a board member coming in, it's essential to assess the company before you even accept your place on the board. It's crucial to assess what the company is saying publicly, compared to what it is actually doing in practice."

–*Dr. Bronwyn King, Australian radiation oncologist; CEO, Tobacco Free Portfolios*

"The future is going to be very interesting for some of these dinosaur boards. If they refuse to change, just like the dinosaurs, they're going to become extinct."

–Wes Hall, executive chair, Kingsdale Advisors

Board Exercise

Each chapter of this book ends with ten questions designed to test board directors' insight, oversight, and foresight on the issue discussed in that chapter.

Once you have answered the questions, give an overall 1 to 10 (1 being poor and 10 being best in class) rating on how well you think your board is dealing with that particular issue. Each of your board colleagues should do the same.

COMPETENT BOARDS SELF-ASSESSMENT TOOL

Using an 11-point spider-web graph, mark each person's score for each issue. The completed diagram (figure E.1) will show whether, and where, directors are aligned in their views, and how well they believe the various issues are being tackled by their board. Analyzing the collective answers to each question should indicate how successfully the board is grappling with the critical issues that confront it, and hopefully generate some ideas for improvement.

For more guidelines and help with this tool, go to:

www.competentboards.com

FIGURE E.1

Example: Recording of individual director's 1-to-10 rating of performance on 11 critical issues facing boards and the corporations they serve (for ease of illustration, only 5 board directors are indicated). Correlation to respective chapters in the book is included.

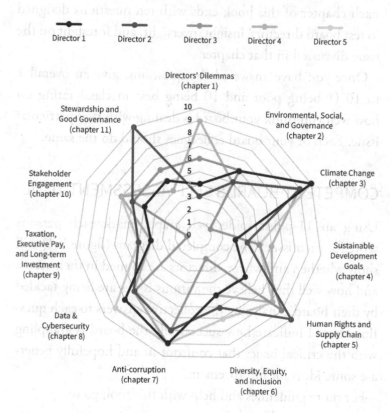

Source: Competent Boards.

Notes

All direct quotes and attributions without specific citations are drawn from interviews conducted by the author up to July 2021. Each individual's affiliations are listed for identification purposes only. Further details about the interviewees, all of whom are members of Competent Boards's faculty, can be found at www.competentboards.com/pages/leaders-archive.

1. Meadows, D., J. Randers, and W. Behrens III. (1972). *The Limits to Growth*. New York: Penguin Publishing.

2. The Sustainability Board Report. (2020). *The Sustainability Board Report 2020*. https://www.boardreport.org/reports-research (accessed July 21, 2021)

3. Edgecliffe-Johnson, A. (2021, June 3). "Why Executives Should Always Listen to Unreasonable Activists." *Financial Times*. https://www.ft.com/content/0bce654c-74bd-47eb-aed4-4c9a8e065467 (accessed July 22, 2021)

4. Mooney, A. (2021, July 6). "Investment Industry at 'Tipping Point' as $43tn in Funds Commit to Net Zero." *Financial Times*. https://www.ft.com/content/e943869b-7afd-4eea-8e0c-6ba3991bc5e3 (accessed July 22, 2021)

5. Rauwald, C. (2021, June 9). "VW Claws Back $351 Million in Diesel-Scandal Damages Deal" *Bloomberg*.

https://www.bloomberg.com/news/articles/2021-06-09/
vw-claws-back-351-million-in-diesel-scandal-damages-deal
(accessed September 24, 2021)

6. Deloitte. (2020). "On the Audit Committee's Agenda:
Defining the Role of the Audit Committee in Overseeing
ESG." Deloitte/Center for Board Effectiveness.
https://www2.deloitte.com/content/dam/Deloitte/fi/
Documents/risk/us-november-OTACA-final.pdf (accessed
July 12, 2021)

7. Benefit Corporation. (n.d.). "State by State Status of
Legislation." https://benefitcorp.net/policymakers/state-by-
state-status (accessed July 21, 2021)

8. The Copenhagen Charter: A Management Guide to
Stakeholder Reporting. (1999). Copenhagen: House of
Mandag Morgen. http://base.socioeco.org/docs/doc-822_
en.pdf (accessed July 22, 2021)

9. McKinsey & Company & FCLTGlobal. (2020, October).
Corporate Long-Term Behaviors: How CEOs and Boards
Drive Sustained Value Creation. https://www.fcltglobal.org/
resource/corporate-long-term-behaviors/ (accessed July 12,
2021)

10. FCLTGlobal. (2019). "The Long-term Habits of a Highly
Effective Corporate Board." https://www.fcltglobal.org/
wp-content/uploads/long-term-habits-of-highly-effective-
corporate-boards.pdf (accessed July 12, 2021)

11. Ibid.

12. Duncan, E. (2021, July 20). "BlackRock Cites Corporate
Governance 'Concerns' for Voting Against 10% of Directors'
Elections." Investment Week. https://www.investmentweek.

co.uk/news/4034687/blackrock-cites-corporate-governance-concerns-voting-directors-elections (accessed July 22, 2021)

13. Whelan, T. (2021). "US Corporate Boards Suffer from Inadequate Expertise in Financially Material ESG Matters." *SSRN Electronic Journal.* https://papers.ssrn.com/sol3/papers.cfm?abstract_id=3758584 (September 24, 2021)

14. Ibid.

15. Fink, L. (2020). "A Fundamental Reshaping of Finance." *BlackRock.* www.blackrock.com/ch/individual/en/larry-fink-ceo-letter (accessed July 22, 2021)

16. Business Roundtable. (2019). "Business Roundtable Redefines the Purpose of a Corporation to Promote 'An Economy that Serves All Americans.'" https://www.businessroundtable.org/business-roundtable-redefines-the-purpose-of-a-corporation-to-promote-an-economy-that-serves-all-americans (accessed July 22, 2021)

17. Schwab, K. (2019). "Why We Need the 'Davos Manifesto' for a Better Kind of Capitalism." *World Economic Forum.* www.weforum.org/agenda/2019/12/why-we-need-the-davos-manifesto-for-better-kind-of-capitalism/ (accessed July 22, 2021)

18. Whitcomb, D. (2020, June 16). "PG&E Pleads Guilty to 84 Counts of Involuntary Manslaughter in California Wildfire." *Reuters.* www.reuters.com/article/us-california-wildfires-pg-e-idUSKBN23N35T (accessed July 26, 2021)

19. Mirchandani, B. (2021). "What You Need to Know about the 2021 Proxy Season." *Forbes.* https://www.forbes.com/sites/bhaktimirchandani/2021/06/28/what-you-need-to-know-about-the-2021-proxy-season/?sh=d1575c67f5e1 (accessed July 26, 2021)

20. Ward-Brennan, M. (2021, July 8). "E&S Proposals Build Momentum this Proxy Season." *Corporate Secretary.* https://www.corporatesecretary.com/articles/esg/32637/es-proposals-build-momentum-proxy-season (accessed July 26, 2021)

21. Hiller, J., and S. Herbst-bayliss. (2021, June 2). "Engine No. 1 Extends Gains with a Third Seat on Exxon Board." *Reuters.* www.reuters.com/business/energy/engine-no-1-win-third-seat-exxon-board-based-preliminary-results-2021-06-02/ (accessed July 29, 2021)

22. Ward-Brennan, M. (2021, July 8). "E&S Proposals Build Momentum this Proxy Season." *Corporate Secretary.* https://www.corporatesecretary.com/articles/esg/32637/es-proposals-build-momentum-proxy-season (accessed July 26, 2021)

23. Hiller, J., and S. Herbst-bayliss. (2021, June 2). "Engine No. 1 Extends Gains with a Third Seat on Exxon Board." *Reuters.* www.reuters.com/business/energy/engine-no-1-win-third-seat-exxon-board-based-preliminary-results-2021-06-02/ (accessed July 29, 2021)

24. Impact Management Project, World Economic Forum, & Deloitte. (2020). "Reporting on Enterprise Value: Illustrated with a Prototype Climate-Related Financial Disclosure Standard." https://29kjwb3armds2g3gi4lq2sx1-wpengine.netdna-ssl.com/wp-content/uploads/Reporting-on-enterprise-value_climate-prototype_Dec20.pdf (accessed July 27, 2021)

25. New Zealand Ministry for the Environment. (2021, April 28). "Mandatory Climate-Related Disclosures." https://environment.govt.nz/what-government-is-doing/areas-of-work/climate-change/mandatory-climate-related-financial-disclosures/ (accessed July 27, 2021)

26. Financial Conduct Authority (Great Britain), Great Britain, Treasury, Great Britain, Department for Business, E. & I. S., Great Britain, & Department for Work and Pensions. (2020). *Interim Report of the UK's Joint Government-Regulator TCFD Taskforce.* https://assets.publishing.service. gov.uk/government/uploads/system/uploads/attachment_data/file/933782/FINAL_TCFD_REPORT.pdf (accessed September 24, 2021)

27. Inditex. (2020). *Inditex Group Annual Report 2020.* https://static.inditex.com/annual_report_2020/assets/pdf/pdfseng/BLOQUES_ING/WE%20REPORT.pdf (accessed September 24, 2021)

28. IPCC. (2021). *Climate Change 2021: The Physical Science Basis. Contribution of Working Group I to the Sixth Assessment Report of the Intergovernmental Panel on Climate Change* [[Masson-Delmotte, V., P. Zhai, A. Pirani, S. L. Connors, C. Péan, S. Berger, N. Caud, Y. Chen, L. Goldfarb, M. I. Gomis, M. Huang, K. Leitzell, E. Lonnoy, J. B. R. Matthews, T. K. Maycock, T. Waterfield, O. Yelekçi, R. Yu and B. Zhou (eds.)]]. Cambridge University Press. In Press.

29. Josephs, J. (2021, April 21). "Climate Change: Shipping Industry Calls for New Global Carbon Tax." *BBC News.* www.bbc.com/news/business-56835352 (accessed July 21, 2021)

30. CDP. (2021). "Putting a Price on Carbon: The State of Internal Carbon Pricing by Corporates Globally." www.cdp. net/en/reports/downloads/5651 (accessed July 15, 2021)

31. World Economic Forum. (2021). *The Global Risks Report 2021.* www.weforum.org/reports/the-global-risks-report-2021/ (accessed July 21, 2021)

32. Murray, J. (2013, October 25). "Investors Demand Fossil Fuel Giants Assess Climate Risks." Business Green. www.businessgreen.com/news/2302927/investors-demand-fossil-fuel-giants-assess-climate-risks (accessed August 25, 2021)

33. Culp, S. (2021, June 29). "Banks Increasingly See Climate Risk as Top Priority." *Forbes*. https://www.forbes.com/sites/steveculp/2021/06/29/banks-increasingly-see-climate-risk-as-top-priority/?sh=52e5a2a58fe5 (accessed September 24, 2021)

34. Task Force on Climate-related Financial Disclosures. (n.d.). "The Use of Scenario Analysis in Disclosure of Climate-related Risks and Opportunities." *TCFD Knowledge Hub*. www.tcfdhub.org/scenario-analysis/ (accessed July 21, 2021)

35. Expert Group on Global Climate Obligations (ed.). (2015). *Oslo Principles on Global Climate Change*. The Hague: Eleven International Publishing.

36. Storebrand. (n.d.). "Our Climate Strategy." www.storebrand.no/en/asset-management/sustainable-investments/our-climate-strategy (accessed July 21, 2021)

37. Boudreau, C. (2021). "Public Promises, Private Lobbying: Investors Want Clarity on Corporate Climate Activity." *Politico*. www.politico.com/news/2021/04/20/investors-corporate-climate-lobbying-activity-483429 (accessed July 21, 2021)

38. The Global Commission on the Economy and Climate. (2018). *Unlocking the Inclusive Growth Story of the 21st Century: Accelerating Climate Action in Urgent Times* (The New Climate Economy Report). https://newclimateeconomy.report/2018/ (accessed July 15, 2021)

39. IEA. (2021). "Net Zero by 2050." https://www.iea.org/reports/net-zero-by-2050 (accessed May 18, 2021)

40. Marsh, A. (2020). "Carney Calls Net-Zero Ambition Great Commercial Opportunity." *Bloomberg.* https://www.bloomberg.com/news/articles/2020-11-09/carney-calls-net-zero-ambition-greatest-commercial-opportunity (accessed July 22, 2021)

41. Crane, D. (2014). "Open Letter from David Crane, CEO of NRG." *Association of Power Producers of Ontario.* https://magazine.appro.org/news/ontario-news/3381-open-letter-from-david-crane-ceo-of-nrg-.html (accessed July 21, 2021)

42. Malik, N., and T. Loh. (2017). "America's Other Coal Job, Ignored by Politicians, Is Dying Fast." *Bloomberg.* www.bloomberg.com/news/articles/2017-08-10/america-s-other-coal-job-ignored-by-politicians-is-dying-fast (accessed July 21, 2021)

43. NRG Energy Inc. (2017, February 28). "NRG Energy (NRG) Q4 2016 Results—Earnings Call Transcript." *Seeking Alpha.* https://seekingalpha.com/article/4050498-nrg-energy-nrg-q4-2016-results-earnings-call-transcript (accessed August 25, 2021)

44. Di Christopher, T. (2017, July 18). "How a Billionaire Hedge Fund Manager Plans to Transform the Biggest American Power Producer Without Getting Burned." *CNBC.* www.cnbc.com/2017/07/18/paul-singer-nrg-turnaround.html (accessed July 21, 2021)

45. Langford, C. (2019). "Houston — Houston? — Becomes a Leader in Renewable Energy." *Courthouse News Service.* www.courthousenews.com/houston-houston-becomes-a-leader-in-renewable-energy/ (accessed July 21, 2021)

46. NRG Energy Inc. (2020). *2020 Sustainability Report*. www. nrg.com/sustainability/progress.html (accessed July 15, 2021)

47. IPCC. (2021). *Climate Change 2021: The Physical Science Basis. Contribution of Working Group I to the Sixth Assessment Report of the Intergovernmental Panel on Climate Change* [[Masson-Delmotte, V., P. Zhai, A. Pirani, S. L. Connors, C. Péan, S. Berger, N. Caud, Y. Chen, L. Goldfarb, M. I. Gomis, M. Huang, K. Leitzell, E. Lonnoy, J. B. R. Matthews, T. K. Maycock, T. Waterfield, O. Yelekçi, R. Yu and B. Zhou (eds.)]]. Cambridge University Press. In Press.

48. United Nations. (n.d.). "THE 17 GOALS | Sustainable Development." https://sdgs.un.org/goals (accessed August 23, 2021)

49. Business & Sustainable Development Commission. (2017). "Valuing the SDG Prize: Unlocking Business Opportunities to Accelerate Sustainable and Inclusive Growth." http:// s3.amazonaws.com/aws-bsdc/Valuing-the-SDG-Prize.pdf (accessed July 13, 2021)

50. Winston, A. (2020, December). "How Did Business's Role in Society Change in 2020?" *Harvard Business Review.* https://hbr.org/2020/12/how-did-businesss-role-in-society-change-in-2020 (accessed July 29, 2021)

51. L'Oreal. (2021). "L'Oréal Suppliers: How We Build Long-term Partnership." www.loreal.com/en/audiences/suppliers/ (accessed July 16, 2021)

52. Sedex (website). (n.d.). "Become a Responsible Business with Sedex". www.sedex.com/ (accessed July 30, 2021)

53. Sharma, D., and F. Kaps. (2021). "Human Rights Due Diligence Legislation in Europe – Implications for Supply Chains to India and South Asia." *DLA Piper.* www. dlapiper.com/en/morocco/insights/publications/2021/03/

human-rights-due-diligence-legislation-in-europe/ (accessed July 21, 2021)

54. Business & Human Rights Resource Centre. (2021). "France's Duty of Vigilance Law." https://www.business-humanrights.org/en/latest-news/frances-duty-of-vigilance-law/ (accessed July 21, 2021)

55. Yadav, M. (2021). "Germany Cabinet Launches Bill to Strengthen Rights Protection in Global Supply Chains." *Jurist.* https://www.jurist.org/news/2021/03/germany-cabinet-launches-bill-to-strengthen-rights-protection-in-global-supply-chains// (accessed July 21, 2021)

56. Kippenberg, J. (2019, June 4). "Netherlands Takes Big Step Toward Tackling Child Labor." *Human Rights Watch.* www.hrw.org/news/2019/06/04/netherlands-takes-big-step-toward-tackling-child-labor (accessed July 21, 2021)

57. Office of the Attorney General, California Department of Justice. (2015, March 31). *The California Transparency in Supply Chains Act.* https://oag.ca.gov/SB657 (accessed August 25, 2021)

58. Burns, P., B. Cacic, K. Contini, T. Grimmer, A. Haque, F. Richmond, J. Rotondi, E. Kim Shin, and G. Stuart. (2021). "UK, US and Canadian Governments Announce New Measures over Alleged Xinjiang, China Human Rights Concerns." *Baker McKenzie.* https://supplychaincompliance.bakermckenzie.com/2021/02/18/uk-us-and-canadian-governments-announce-new-measures-over-alleged-xinjiang-china-human-rights-concerns/ (accessed July 21, 2021)

59. Equator Principles. (2021). "EP Association Members & Reporting—The Equator Principles." www.equator-principles.com/members-reporting/ (accessed July 21, 2021)

60. Palma, S. (2021, June 17). "US Import Ban Bursts Top Glove Bubble." *Financial Times*. https://www.ft.com/content/1f0634c0-8916-442b-a06a-ecde5507d2ea (accessed July 21, 2021)

61. Dixon-Fyle, S., K. Dolan, V. Hunt, and S. Prince. (2020). "How Diversity & Inclusion Matter." *McKinsey & Company*. https://www.mckinsey.com/featured-insights/diversity-and-inclusion/diversity-wins-how-inclusion-matters (accessed July 16, 2021)

62. Catalyst. (2019). "The Bottom Line: Connecting Corporate Performance and Gender Diversity." https://www.catalyst.org/wp-content/uploads/2019/01/The_Bottom_Line_Connecting_Corporate_Performance_and_Gender_Diversity.pdf (accessed July 16, 2021)

63. Hewlett, S., M. Marshall, L. Sherbin, and T. Gon-salves. (2020). "Innovation, Diversity, and Market Growth." *Coqual*. https://coqual.org/wp-content/uploads/2020/09/31_innovationdiversityandmarketgrowth_keyfindings-1.pdf (accessed July 16, 2021)

64. Cloverpop. (2018). "White Paper: Hacking Diversity with Inclusive Decision Making from Cloverpop." www.cloverpop.com/hacking-diversity-with-inclusive-decision-making-white-paper (accessed July 16, 2021)

65. Smith, J. (2021). "What Investors Expect from the 2021 Proxy Season." *EY*. www.ey.com/en_us/board-matters/what-investors-expect-from-the-2021-proxy-season (accessed July 16, 2021)

66. Isidore, C. (2020). "Nasdaq to Corporate America: Make Your Boards More Diverse or Get Out." *CNN*. https://

www.cnn.com/2020/12/01/investing/nasdaq-rule-board-of-directors-diversity/index.html (accessed July 21, 2021)

67. Canadian Gender & Good Governance Alliance. (2018). "Directors' Playbook." https://irp-cdn.multiscreensite.com/df49ced3/files/uploaded/Gender%20%20Good%20Governance%20Playbook%20-%20English_WEB_v2.pdf (accessed July 21, 2021)

68. Equality and Human Rights Commission. (2014). "Good Equality Practice for Employers: Equality Policies, Equality Training and Monitoring," p. 89.

69. Spencer Stuart. (2020). "2020 US Spencer Stuart Board Index," p. 58. https://www.spencerstuart.com/-/media/2020/december/ssbi2020/2020_us_spencer_stuart_board_index.pdf (accessed July 15, 2021)

70. PwC. (2018). "Board Composition: Consider the Value of Younger Directors on Your Board." https://www.pwc.dk/da/publikationer/2018/pwc-census-of-younger-directors-consider-the-value-for-your-board.pdf (accessed July 16, 2021)

71. State Street Global Advisors. (2020). "Diversity Strategy, Goals & Disclosure: Our Expectations for Public Companies." https://www.ssga.com/library-content/pdfs/global/letterhead_racial_equity_guidance.pdf (accessed July 22, 2021)

72. State Street Global Advisors. (2021). "CEO's Letter on Our 2021 Proxy Voting Agenda." https://www.ssga.com/international/en/institutional/ic/insights/ceo-letter-2021-proxy-voting-agenda (accessed July 22, 2021)

73. Catalyst. (2020). "Pyramid: Women in S&P 500 Companies." https://www.catalyst.org/research/women-ceos-of-the-sp-500/ (accessed July 16, 2021)

74. PwC. (2020). "Insights from PwC's 2020 Annual Corporate Directors Survey." https://www.pwc.com/us/en/services/governance-insights-center/library/annual-corporate-directors-survey.html (accessed July 16, 2021)

75. Integrity Initiatives International. (n.d.). "Declaration in Support of the Creation of an International Anti-Corruption Court. Integrity Initiatives International." www.integrityinitiatives.org/declaration (accessed July 19, 2021)

76. KPMG Australia. (2021). "Fraud Survey 2021." https://home.kpmg/au/en/home/insights/2021/03/fraud-risk-survey-2021.html (accessed July 22, 2021)

77. Jha, C.K., and S. Sarangi. (2018). "Women and Corruption: What Positions Must They Hold to Make a Difference?" *Journal of Economic Behavior & Organization* 151: 219–233. https://doi.org/10.1016/j.jebo.2018.03.021 (accessed July 21, 2021); Baur, M., N. Charron, and L. Wängnerud. (2018). "Close the Political Gender Gap to Reduce Corruption." *U4 Anti-Corruption Resource Centre.* https://www.u4.no/publications/close-the-political-gender-gap-to-reduce-corruption (accessed July 21, 2021); United Nations Office on Drugs and Crime. (2019). "Corruption and Gender: Women and Men Affected Differently by Corruption, but No Evidence Women or Men Are Less Corruptible." www.unodc.org/lpo-brazil/en/frontpage/2019/12/corruption-and-gender_-women-and-men-affected-differently-by-corruption--but-no-evidence-women-or-men-are-less-corruptible.html (accessed July 21, 2021)

78. OECD. (2020). "Corporate Anti-Corruption Compliance Drivers, Mechanisms, and Ideas for Change," p. 96. https://

www.oecd.org/daf/anti-bribery/Corporate-anti-corruption-compliance-drivers-mechanisms-and-ideas-for-change.pdf (accessed July 22, 2021)

79. Global Compact Network Canada. (2017). "Designing an Anti-Corruption Compliance Program: A Guide for Canadian Businesses." https://globalcompact.ca/designing-an-anti-corruption-compliance-program-a-guide-for-canadian-businesses/ (accessed July 22, 2021)

80. International Chamber of Commerce. (2017). "ICC Business Integrity Compendium 2017." https://iccwbo.org/publication/icc-business-integrity-compendium-2017/ (accessed July 21, 2021)

81. OECD. (2014). *OECD Foreign Bribery Report: An Analysis of the Crime of Bribery of Foreign Public Officials.* https://www.oecd-ilibrary.org/governance/oecd-foreign-bribery-report_9789264226616-en (accessed July 19, 2021)

82. Ponemon Institute LLC. (2017). "The Impact of Data Breaches on Reputation & Share Value." *Centrify.* https://www.centrify.com/media/4772757/ponemon_data_breach_impact_study_uk.pdf (accessed July 19, 2021)

83. FTI Consulting. (2020). "Corporate Data Privacy Today: A Look at the Current State of Readiness, Perception and Compliance." https://static2.ftitechnology.com/docs/white-papers/FTI%20Consulting%20White%20Paper%20-%20Corporate%20Data%20Privacy%20Today.pdf (accessed July 19, 2021)

84. Simmons, D. (2021, January 12). "13 Countries with GDPR-like Data Privacy Laws." *Comforte.* https://insights.comforte.com/13-countries-with-gdpr-like-data-privacy-laws

(accessed August 25, 2021); Woodward, M. (2021, July 8). "16 Countries with GDPR-like Data Privacy Laws." *SecurityScorecard*. https://securityscorecard.com/blog/countries-with-gdpr-like-data-privacy-laws (accessed August 25, 2021)

85. OECD. (2021). "Base Erosion and Profit Shifting—OECD BEPS." www.oecd.org/tax/beps/ (accessed July 20, 2021)

86. Willis Towers Watson. (2021). *ESG and Executive Compensation: Hearing from Board Members Globally.* p. 37. https://www.willistowerswatson.com/-/media/WTW/Insights/2021/04/ESG-and-Executive-Compensation-Report-2021.pdf?modified=20210419083740 (accessed July 20, 2021)

87. Economic Policy Institute. (2019). "CEO Compensation Has Grown 940% Since 1978: Typical Worker Compensation Has Risen Only 12% During that Time." www.epi.org/publication/ceo-compensation-2018/ (accessed July 20, 2021)

88. Kharif, O. (2020, July 20). "Electronic Arts Executive Pay Draws Fire from Proxy Advisers." *Bloomberg.* www.bloomberg.com/news/articles/2020-07-20/electronic-arts-executive-pay-draws-fire-from-proxy-advisers (accessed August 23, 2021)

89. A4S CFO Leadership Network. (2016). "Essential Guide to Capex: A Practical Guide to Embedding Sustainability into Capital Investment Appraisal." https://www.accountingforsustainability.org/content/dam/a4s/corporate/home/KnowledgeHub/Guide-pdf/The%20A4S%20Essential%20Guide%20to%20Capex.pdf.downloadasset.pdf

90. Marcario, R. (2018). "Our Urgent Gift to the Planet." *LinkedIn.* www.linkedin.com/pulse/our-urgent-gift-planet-rose-marcario/ (accessed July 22, 2021)

91. Baptist World Aid Australia. (2019). *The 2019 Ethical Fashion Report: The Truth behind the Barcode.* https://media.business-humanrights.org/media/documents/files/documents/FashionReport_2019_9-April-19-FINAL.pdf (accessed July 21, 2021)

92. Roundtable on Sustainable Palm Oil (website). (n.d.). https://rspo.org/ (accessed July 21, 2021)

93. Ørsted. (2020). "Our Green Build-out." https://orsted.com/en/sustainability/climate-action-plan/our-green-build-out (accessed July 22, 2021)

94. Morris, R. (2018). "From Fossil Fuels to Green Energy: The Ørsted Story." *London Business School.* https://www.london.edu/think/iie-from-fossil-fuels-to-green-energy-the-orsted-story (accessed July 22, 2021)

95. Ørsted. (2021). "Shares." https://orsted.com/en/investors/shares (accessed July 22, 2021)

96. Reuters. (2020, March 18). "Orsted, TEPCO to Jointly Bid for Offshore Wind Power Project in Chiba." *Reuters.* www.reuters.com/article/orsted-windpower-japan-tep-hldg-idAFL4N2BB2NG (accessed July 22, 2021)

97. Ørsted. (2021). "Climate Targets—Reaching Net Zero & Beyond." https://orsted.com/en/sustainability/climate-action-plan/reducing-our-emissions (accessed July 22, 2021)

98. Ørsted. (2021). "Three in a Row: Ørsted Again Ranked World's Most Sustainable Energy Company." https://orsted.tw/en/news/2021/01/most-sustainable-energy-company-2021 (accessed July 22, 2021)

99. Kinkead, G., and E. Gunn. (1999, May 24). "In the Future, People Like Me Will Go to Jail; Ray Anderson Is on a Mission to Clean Up American Businesses—Starting with His Own. Can a Georgia Carpet Mogul Save the Planet?" *Fortune.* https://money.cnn.com/magazines/fortune/fortune_archive/1999/05/24/260285/index.htm (accessed July 30, 2021)

100. Securities Commission Malaysia. (2021). *Malaysian Code on Corporate Governance*, p. 68. https://www.sc.com.my/api/documentms/download.ashx?id=239e5ea1-a258-4db8-a9e2-41c215bdb776 (accessed July 29, 2021)

101. Edelman. (2021). "2021 Edelman Trust Barometer." https://www.edelman.com/trust/2021-trust-barometer (accessed July 21, 2021)

102. Bank Jorgensen, H., and T. Bryant. (2020). *Future Boardroom Competencies: 2020 Report.* Toronto: Competent Boards. https://competentboards.com/news-views/

103. UBS. (2021). "UBS Investor Watch: With Renewed Purpose, Investors Plan to Use Their Capital to Drive Change after COVID-19." https://www.ubs.com/global/en/media/display-page-ndp/en-20210602-ubs-investor-watch.html (accessed July 22, 2021)

104. Cain, K., M. Lipton, S. Rosenblum, and W. Savitt. (2020, May 27). "On the Purpose of the Corporation." *The Harvard Law School Forum on Corporate Governance.* https://corpgov.law.harvard.edu/2020/05/27/on-the-purpose-of-the-corporation/ (accessed July 21, 2021)

105. Bank Jorgensen, H., and T. Bryant. (2020). *Future Boardroom Competencies: 2020 Report.* Toronto: Competent Boards.

106. Ibid.

Index

About the Author

Helle Bank Jorgensen is an internationally recognized expert on sustainable business practices, with a 30-year record of turning environmental, social, and governance (ESG) risks into innovative and profitable business opportunities. She works with many global Fortune 500 board members and executives, as well as smaller companies and investors.

Helle is the founder and chief executive of Competent Boards, which offers online climate and ESG programs that draw on the experience of over 100 renowned board members, executives, and investors. Hundreds of directors and senior executives have enrolled in these programs to mitigate the risks and seize the opportunities presented by ESG, especially climate change.

Helle is an expert advisor to the World Economic Forum, and The Prince's Accounting for Sustainability Project, and serves as a Nasdaq Center for Board Excellence Insights Council Member. She has served as the Chair of the European Sustainability Reporting Association (ESRA), the Global Compact Network Canada, Datamaran, and as a member of the Sustainability Advisory Panel of the American Institute of Certified Public Accountants (AICPA), and the Sustainability Policy Group of the Institute of European Accountants (FEE).

She trained as a business lawyer and state-authorized public accountant in Denmark, and holds a master's degree in business administration and auditing. She is a former PwC audit and advisory partner in Denmark and the United States, leading the firm's sustainability and climate practices.

Helle has pioneered corporate reporting of ESG as part of the widening recognition that environmental, social, and governance issues are a crucial contributor to any organization's success—or failure. She created the world's first "green account" based on lifecycle assessment, and the first integrated annual report that combines ESG with financial performance. She has worked on natural capital accounting for the International Finance Corporation and the World Bank.

In 2020 she was awarded the Global Impact Award and named one of "5 people in ESG to look out for." She is a regular keynote speaker and author of many thought-leading articles.

Helle currently lives in Toronto. When she is not keeping watch over ESG, she enjoys bicycling, kayaking, and hiking with her husband.